Disillusioned
Malaise

An Analysis of Discord…

By Michael Bennett

Published by:
The Professional Image, Inc.
In the US: South Beach and South Florida
International: St. Croix, St. Thomas, Tortola
Contact us at: foodbrat@gmail.com

ISBN: 978-1-66640-636-8

Thanks to our Staff:
SENIOR Editor: Eileen Clark
ASSISTANT EDITOR: JESS "E"
Photographers: The Professional Image, Inc.

The Professional Image, Inc.
~South Florida~
96401 Overseas Hwy. | Key Largo, Fl. 33037 | 305.799.8305

Ordering Information:

Quantity sales: Special discounts are available on quantity purchases by corpo-rations, associations, and others. For details, contact the publisher at the address above.

Orders by U.S. trade bookstores and wholesalers. Please contact TPI

Forward:

This Book's Viewpoint:

Disillusionment arises when life experiences strongly invalidate pragmatic assumptions or deeply held beliefs. Under these conditions, people feel lost, confused, and disconnected from their social environments.

Disillusion comes from within ... from the failure of some dear and secret hope. The world makes no promises; we only dream it does; and when we wake, we cry!

Pearl Mary Teresa Craigie

What is American disillusionment?

"What happened to the American Dream—and who destroyed it?"

- I promise a search for culprits and causes.
- From Carter to Biden: How We Lost Faith in the Future.
- The two eras are linked to highlight a recurring crisis of confidence.
  - This is not merely political—it is also personal. Disillusionment exists not only in Washington but also in our homes.
- Personalizes the theme to make it resonate beyond policy.
- Can we still turn around a country that was founded on hope but is now operating on fumes?
  - This implies an urgency we need to bear in mind while leaving room for a hopeful future payoff.
- Why Americans feel worse off—even when the numbers say they shouldn't.
  - This book will dig into emotional and psychological truths, not just stats.

- The rhetoric of unity, the reality of division: A decline in trust over forty years.
  - This taps into the tension between political and media messaging and true, lived experiences.
- We've been here before. So why didn't we learn from it?
  - I try to explore my curiosities by pointing out historical repetition.
- Your disillusionment is a warning, not a failure.
  - By reading this, your feelings are validated and elevated to a national signal.
- Change was promised. What you got was chaos.
- I did not expect to see the reflection of America's soul in the mirror. By highlighting these facts, I aim to evoke depth and provoke reflection, appealing to contemplative readers.

Our mental state as a Nation can be thought of as a nationwide culture of "Anomie"

Anomie can be a life-altering disruption in the life of an individual or it can be a disruption in the culture of a whole society — or both. The state of the individual subjected to a double bind situation in the psych lab or to a cultural dilemma has been distinguished from the causal state of anomie and labeled "anomie".

These are examples of when a culture is disrupted and loses cohesion—when there are conflicting or absent "norms." Contact situations by definition require an assimilation process that can take generations.

The described process of adjustment is basically similar in case after case and usually dire. Large waves of migrants or refugees also necessitate cultural adjustments in the receiving society.

....Wars, famines, pandemics, economic crises, the introduction of disruptive new technologies, all require major cultural adaptations.

.... Any one of these can become stressful for individuals. A society of such stressed individuals impedes cultural adjustment.

This weakens the social fabric and exacerbates the political fragmentation we are currently experiencing.

The state of anomie can be frustrating, even life-threatening. An initial reaction is to identify someone with the authority to take care of what feels disturbing. This is a passive reaction leading to apathy.

However, the relationship between culture and society is a two-way street.

.... In the past, societies have not had the conceptual tools to plan for adaptation in disruptive circumstances and to guide cultural change toward satisfactory ends.

Many Americans coped with the current ailments by turning inward. Outlandish fashion and outrageous fads such as streaking, mood rings, and pet rocks became common. Younger Americans finished their workweeks and sought escape in discotheques. Controversy surrounding "decaying morality" surfaced with regard to increased drug use, sexual promiscuity, and a rising divorce rate. As a result, a powerful religious movement turned political in the hopes of changing directions toward a more innocent time.

This led to the formulation of the "Me Generation".

Disillusioned Malaise

An Analysis of Discord:

Table of Contents:

Introduction:

I am writing this as a tool to help me align my lifelong feelings of futility.

As others do at this point in their life, I have recently reminisced about my youth. I have always felt young. However, as a Baby Boomer, I find that my age has become a disadvantage in pursuing a career typically associated with younger individuals.

Initially, this book felt entirely outside my expertise. However, I felt comfortable committing to the task of writing a sociological reflection on the events that have shaped my lifetime. It is wonderful to see how others have articulated this story with such clarity. Their ability to convey the narrative so effectively is truly admirable.

I want to present the Bureaucratic Machine:
Government Waste and Duplication.

The federal government operates hundreds of programs with overlapping missions, leading to massive inefficiency and waste, including:

- 342 economic development programs
- 130 programs for the disabled
- 90 early childhood development programs
- 75 programs for international education and training
- 72 safe water programs
- Cost to Taxpayers

Duplicative and overlapping programs cost taxpayers hundreds of billions of dollars annually, with estimates of at least $364.5 billion in spending every year on such programs. The Government Accountability Office (GAO) reports that addressing these inefficiencies could save over $100 billion in the next decade.

Examples of Waste:

Two separate agencies inspect the same type of catfish, duplicating both effort and cost.

- There are 45 programs in nine agencies for employment of people with disabilities, and over 90 programs to promote green buildings.
- In one case, $2.6 million was spent on a program intended to train Chinese sex workers in responsible alcohol consumption while working.

Missed Opportunities for Reform:

Since 2011, the GAO has made hundreds of recommendations to eliminate waste, but only about 37% have been implemented, resulting in $20 billion in savings—far less than what is possible.

- Unspent funds, known as obligated balances, reached $870 billion in 2014, highlighting further inefficiency.

Finally:

The federal bureaucracy is riddled with duplication, overlap, and fragmentation, costing taxpayers billions each year. Despite repeated calls for reform and clear recommendations, much of this waste persists due to slow implementation and entrenched interests.

My adulthood began during a tumultuous period—the 1960s, both in the United States and globally..

...The U.S. witnessed the assassinations of prominent figures, including President John F. Kennedy, Senator Robert F. Kennedy, and Dr. Martin Luther King Jr.

...The country also became embroiled in the Vietnam War, with U.S. troop involvement peaking in 1968 at over 600,000 combat soldiers—many of whom were draftees.

...A burgeoning counterculture movement emerged as the Baby Boom generation came of age.

...Crime spiked across the country, even amid economic improvement.

....In this backdrop former Vice President Richard Nixon was elected President in 1968 on a platform of cracking down on crime and ending the war in Vietnam.

Nixon substantially reduced the number of U.S. troops in Vietnam and ended the military draft in 1973. However, Nixon also escalated bombing of Cambodia and Laos without Congressional approval. The U.S., South Vietnam, and North Vietnam all agreed to end the war in the Paris Peace Accords in 1973.

Many Americans felt deceived about the causes and conduct of the war, and disillusioned by the more than 50,000 American deaths.

After President Ford lost the election by a narrow margin... President Carter aimed to elevate human rights to the top of his agenda and sought a series of new agreements with the Soviet Union.

However, Carter's vision was largely undermined by political and economic realities. The Economy remained weak and deficit spending and the end of the peg of the U.S. dollar to gold led to massive inflation and slow growth ...a phenomenon referred to as "stagflation."

The End of the Malaise...
President Carter faced a strong primary challenge from Massachusetts Senator Ted Kennedy. Carter eventually won but the wound between the two did not heal during the election season. Carter was faced in the general election by Republican former California Governor Ronald Reagan.

- When Reagan took office, a series of events contributed to the end of the malaise period.
- Massive tax cuts began to spur the economy. Furthermore,

- Reagan's defense buildup restored American confidence against the Soviet Union.
- On Inauguration Day in January 1981, Iran released the American hostages.
- Oil prices cratered during a large glut in the 1980s, causing a sharp decline in Soviet finances. Resistance to the Soviets in Afghanistan became more resolute and led to the eventual Soviet withdrawal in 1989.
- For many Americans, the dark period of the 1970s appeared to be over. As stated in the 1984 presidential campaign, "It's morning in America again."

Thinking about what America should be:

Describing "American greatness" is inherently subjective and can vary widely depending on individual perspectives, values, and historical interpretations. However, several key themes and characteristics are commonly associated with the concept of American greatness.

Our Historical Achievements:

Founding Principles: The ideals of liberty, democracy, and the rule of law as articulated in foundational documents like the *Declaration of Independence* and the Constitution represent a commitment to individual rights and governance by consent of the governed.

Civil Rights Progress: Throughout history, movements advocating for civil rights, *gender equality*, and social justice have transformed American society, reflecting a pursuit of greater equality and inclusion.

Our Economic Innovation:

Our instinctual Entrepreneurial Spirit: The U.S. has a rich history of innovation and entrepreneurship, with a culture that encourages creativity and risk-taking. This spirit has led to breakthroughs in technology, industry, and business that have driven economic growth.

America's strength lies in its identity as a cultural melting pot. As one of the largest economies in the world, America's economic influence has shaped global markets and trade relationships, making significant contributions to both domestic prosperity and global development.

Cultural Influences:

Diverse Cultural Contributions: American culture, encompassing music, art, literature, and entertainment, has had a significant impact worldwide. Artistic genres like jazz, rock, hip-hop, and film have become global phenomena.

America is stronger as a Cultural Melting Pot: The blending of diverse cultures, traditions, and ideas from immigrants and communities has enriched American society, fostering creativity and innovation.

Scientific and Technological Advances:

The U.S. continues to pioneer research in numerous scientific fields: The U.S. has been at the forefront of scientific and technological advancements, including space exploration, medicine, and information technology, contributing to global knowledge and progress.

Innovation Hubs: Institutions like Silicon Valley have established the U.S. as a leader in technology and innovation, transforming industries and shaping the future.

Global leadership has often been American-led:

International Institutions: The United States has played a pivotal role in establishing and supporting international organizations such as the United Nations, NATO, and the World Bank, promoting global stability, security, and development.

Peaceful Humanitarian Efforts: Through international aid and development programs, the United States has contributed to addressing global challenges such as poverty, disease, and armed conflict

Resilience and Adaptability:

Overcoming Challenges: Our history is marked by resilience in the face of challenges, including world wars, global economic downturns, and nationally-based social upheaval. The ability to adapt and evolve in response to changing circumstances showcases the strength of American character.

Commitment to Improvement: The ongoing pursuit of a "more perfect union" reflects a commitment to addressing social issues, inequality, and injustice, underlining the belief in progress.

Democratic Values:

Commitment to American Democracy: The establishment and preservation of democratic principles, including free and fair elections, freedom of speech, and the right to assemble, underscore America's commitment to representative governance.

Civil Society: A robust civil society, characterized by a range of civic organizations, activist movements, and a vibrant public discourse, is seen as essential to the health of democracy and the pursuit of collective goals.

Hopefully Next:

American greatness encompasses a complex interplay of historical achievements, cultural contributions, economic innovation, and a commitment to democratic values and human rights. It reflects both the accomplishments of the nation and the ongoing struggles to live up to its ideals. While interpretations of what constitutes "greatness" may differ, there is a common thread of aspiration towards progress, opportunity, and a better future for all.

Priorities of my dialog:

The results of my decades of Malaise are seen so regularly now in America I have decided to turn this book into Volume one of multiple volumes that will explore the intricate tapestry of societal challenges we face today. Each volume will delve into different facets of this malaise, from ...the increasing disconnection among families, fueled by technology. I aim to dissect not only the symptoms but also the underlying causes that have led us here, offering a reflective lens through which we can better understand our current landscape.

I plan to focus on personal narratives and observations that highlight how individuals within our society have navigated their daily lives. By weaving together stories from Americans' individually diverse backgrounds. I hope to illustrate a broader understanding of our shared experiences and resilience. The goal is not merely to lament our posture but to provoke thought about potential pathways onward—inviting readers into a dialogue about mending and renewal.

As I embark on this writing journey, I'm eager for your insights or any themes you think deserve special attention in future volumes. Your perspective would be invaluable as I seek to create a comprehensive exploration that resonates with readers across the generations. Thank you for joining me on this endeavor; together we can shed light on these pressing issues and inspire change.

I have been curious about this since the 1970s when my eyes were opened in college and I noticed what was going on around me and how the world was shifting in both subtle and profound ways. The social movements, the music, the art—all of it seemed to reflect a deep yearning for change. I began to question not just what I was being taught in the classroom, but also the narratives that dominated our culture. How did these shifts shape our identities and influence our values?

As I delved deeper into my studies, books and later electronic media became my refuge—a way to explore different perspectives and understand the intricacies of our societal evolution. Each of life's details offered a piece of a larger puzzle that spanned decades of thought and action; from civil disobediences and rights to womens rights and environmentalism, every movement carried its own weight and significance. Reflecting on those formative years brings back memories of late-night discussions with classmates about everything from politics to philosophy. We were all trying to make sense of an Nova-paced, ever-changing landscape while grappling with our own prevailing beliefs and aspirations. It is fascinating how those feelings still resonate today, prompting me to consider how far we have come—and how much further we still need to go in fostering understanding and progress of our society.

While in college I noticed a heavy bias of most educators toward liberal leanings. I have discerned now that these traits were to get worse through my years in college. So, as I grew, if I noticed them around me I would nudge them out of the way. These years taught me to always constrain modifying people's expectations and desires, it was easy to do being a chef. The creative needs of my teenage self; a fundamentally analytical mind was working towards balancing what was happening to me and around me and what I could change. This was hard to try to do even if you are driven, I could not balance my desire and needs. Having a family, and my grandiose love of being a chef has always kept me from entering into this professional political expanse.

How liberalism devastated America:
The assertion that "liberalism has destroyed America" reflects a specific political viewpoint often associated with criticism of liberal policies and ideologies. Advocates of this perspective argue that certain liberal approaches and policies have led to negative consequences for American society. It's essential to clarify that this view is highly contentious and subjective, and it represents one side of a broader political debate. Here are some arguments often made by critics of liberalism in America:

1. Economic Policies:

Welfare State Expansion: Critics argue that the expansion of welfare programs has created dependency on government assistance, disincentive work and personal responsibility. They contend that such policies have contributed to a culture where individuals rely on government rather than seeking employment and self-sufficiency.

High Taxes and Regulations: Opponents of liberal economic policies often claim that high taxes and extensive regulations stifle economic growth, hurt small businesses, and lead to reduced investment in the economy.

2. Social Issues:

Family Structure: Some critics argue that liberal policies have contributed to the breakdown of traditional family structures. They often cite high divorce rates, single-parent households, and changing gender roles as evidence that liberal social policies have had detrimental effects on the family unit.

Moral Decline: Conservative critics often assert that liberalism has led to a decline in morals and values, influenced by liberal stances on issues such as abortion, drug legalization, and sexual orientation rights. They argue that these changes have contributed to societal instability.

3. Education:

Curriculum Changes: Some critics believe that liberal education policies promote a progressive agenda that undermines traditional educational values. They argue that this includes a focus on identity politics, "political correctness," and a perceived disregard for classical academic standards.

Common Core and Standardization: Opposition to standardized educational initiatives, such as Common Core, is often framed as a liberal overreach in education. Critics argue that these policies can lead to a one-size-fits-all approach that diminishes local control and parental choice.

4. Political Polarization:

Partisan Divide: Critics may argue that the liberal agenda has contributed to increased polarization in American politics. They claim that liberal ideologies promote an "us vs. them" mentality that exacerbates divisions between political parties and reduces the possibility of bipartisan cooperation.

Identity Politics: The focus on identity politics by some liberal factions is seen by critics as a divisive approach that prioritizes individual identity over shared American values, leading to further fragmentation in society.

5. Cultural Impact:

Media and Entertainment: Some argue that liberal influences dominate media and entertainment, promoting a worldview that undermines traditional values and community cohesion. Critics claim that this has led to a culture that trivializes serious issues and promotes destructive behaviors.

Cancel Culture: The rise of "cancel culture" is often attributed to liberalism, with critics asserting that it stifles free speech and shuts down open dialogue and debate.

After all:

It's important to note that the criticisms of liberalism outlined above represent one perspective in a complex and ongoing political discourse. Supporters of liberalism would argue that many of their policies have led to significant progress in civil rights, social justice, public welfare, and economic inclusion. They often contend that such changes address systemic inequities and promote a more just society.

Debates about the effectiveness and consequences of liberal policies are part of the broader democratic process and reflect differing values and beliefs about the role of government, individual responsibility, and social progress. Engaging in constructive dialogue about these issues is crucial for a healthy democracy.

Since the time of secondary school, without reservation, I have believed in our leaders. Knowing the tenacity of America's hatred of war, I never thought about why it always seemed we were fighting one war after another, year after year. It was only through deep reflection that I began to realize the complexities behind these conflicts. The sacrifices made by countless individuals, both military personnel and civilians, weighed heavily on my heart, reminding values of empathy and compassion towards others. me of the profound cost of war. I grew increasingly thankful for those who dedicate their lives to service, often putting their own dreams on hold in the name of duty. Their bravery inspired me to seek a better understanding of our nation's history and the decisions that lead us into conflict and ultimately shaped the path we walk today. I found myself diving into books, documentaries, and discussions that illuminated the complexities of our past. *Each* story, from the struggles for American freedom to the sacrifices made during multiple wartimes, deepened my appreciation for those who fought not just with weapons but with words and ideas. As I explored these narratives, I realized how interconnected our histories are and how they engage and resonate in today's society. The bravery of those who stood up against injustice sparked a desire within me to engage more actively in conversations about peace and unity. It became clear that understanding history is vital—not only to honor those who came before us but also to inspire current and future generations to strive for a world marked by compassion rather than conflict. I am grateful for this journey of discovery; it has opened my eyes to different perspectives and challenged me to think critically about our present circumstances. This newfound awareness motivates me every day as I seek ways to contribute positively within my community. As I delved into various perspectives—from historical accounts to personal narratives—I developed a greater appreciation for peace advocates. This journey has not only shaped my views but also instilled in me a strong desire to contribute positively to society. Whether through volunteering or engaging in community discussions about peace initiatives, I feel compelled to honor those who have fought not just with weapons but with words and ideas for a more harmonious world. Each day presents an opportunity for growth and learning; I am grateful for this path that has allowed me to expand my understanding while embracing the theories.

Once I realized that the big weapon and aircraft manufacturing giants were the actual beneficiaries of being in these wars, it then made more sense to me. Then I questioned who in our government is making a buck because of decisions to send our youth to fight in any particular conflict. As far back as the beginning of the Vietnam War, our youth knew these conflicts benefited a multinational companies more than the alleged people being helped. This came to me, as an awakening in my teenage years.

I now understood that government wasn't always by the people for the people.

My goals became:

(1) Research the economic factors that influenced the United States' involvement in any war especially the Vietnam War.

(2) Investigate the role of multinational corporations and their governmental bourgeois of War, including their enormous potential benefits from the conflict.

(3) Explore criticisms and analyses of potential profiteering by government officials during our Malaise era.

(4) Find information on the concept of the President Eisenhower's "military-industrial complex" and its historical context, particularly in relation to America.

(5) Research historical debates and discussions surrounding the motivations behind the American Malaise, considering perspectives beyond stated objectives.

(6) Investigate government oversight and regulations in place to address potential conflicts of interest related to what we are detailing..

(7) Explore the long-term economic consequences of our malaise for the United States and other involved nations.

(8) Research public opinion and protests related to the idea that socio-economic interests were a primary driver of the strife.

In my past:

This of course has led me to think about my past. I generally felt great about my past, yet things happening around me were telling a different story. "It was the *Best of Times,* it was the *Worst of Times*" might have been the title of this book, because I always lived in a world of creation, one that re-volves around forcing yourself to endure hardship, and hone your passions as you innovate. This is the world of being a chef.

Outside the walls of my culinary haunt, the world didn't determine much in my life. I usually call the shots for myself and sometimes as many as 150 other people that surround me. It came to the point I didn't want to be the one whose decisions affected so many people's lives in every way everyday. I grew to know the pressure of what it was like to be a Presidential-like leader in my small world. My mind always wandered about what I might do in place of this employment position. I have found there has not been anything but, writing to quell my need to be artistic. So this led me to write books. I have six printed books, two ghost-written books, and many published e-books.

Daily in my life, I see the common quintessential citizenry turn apathetic and disengaged, interested only in material things: boasting, gluttonous, and self-obsessed behaviors, yet, not caring for ardent societal issues. This book felt totally out of my wheelhouse, but I feel comfortable telling you that this was an easy decision to jump into the role of writing my sociological take on the happening in my lifetime. This same story has been written about clearly by others. The results of my decades of *Malaise* are seen so regularly now in America I have decided to turn this book into volume one of five volumes in total. I hope you will enjoy it, as this book is intended to be a tool for me to bridge happenings in my life to what might be happening to all of us soon.

I have been curious about our American society since the 1970s, when my eyes were opened in college and noticed what was going on around me. While there I recognized a heavy bias of most educators toward liberal leanings. I have discerned now that these traits were to get worse through my years in college.

So, as I grew, if I noticed them around me I would nudge them out of the way. These years taught me to always constrain modifying people's expectations and desires, it was easy to do, already being a chef. The creative needs of my teenage self; with a fundamentally analytical mind was working towards balancing what was happening to me, the strange things going on around me and, what I could change. This was hard to try to do even if you are driven, I could not balance my desire and needs. Having a family, and my grandiose love of being a chef has always kept me from entering into this professional political expanse.

Since the time of secondary school, without reservation, I have believed in our American leaders. Knowing the tenacity of America's hatred of war, I never thought about why it always seemed we were fighting one war after another, year after year. Once I realized that the big weapon and aircraft manufacturing giants were the actual beneficiaries of being in these wars, it then made more sense to me. Then I questioned who in our government is making a buck because of decisions to send our youth to fight in a particular conflict.

As far back as the beginning of the Vietnam War, our youth knew these conflicts benefited a multinational company more than the alleged people being helped. This came to me, as an awakening in my teenage years, I now understood that government wasn't always by the people for the people.

"Months and years went by. I felt angry for being so powerless over these issues, and I started feeling numb from this growing dilemma. I felt angry about being so powerless..."

The people who fought against the government during the Vietnam War are now older and have the clout to be heard. They have become the source that now amplifies the distrust in American leadership. They carried a burden in their younger lives that became a way of life and later became aggression towards others that didn't have the same life story. They wore their divisiveness on their sleeves as they entered into every election battle. They had a motto, "go after the man". It has been decades that Americans built walls singularly around their separatist morals and did not trust anyone in previous governmental roles opposite of their penchant.

Political radicals knew back then that our country's leadership and their young staff wanted these conflicts to spread. This became a culture within our American Society that has not changed and yet has evolved into "the Swamp" - as President Trump names it, we have today.

Today, after decades, those previous radical bureaucratic staff members are now our current leaders in our government. Those radicals in thought - always contested that If the subject (news) isn't based (fabricated) upon their ideals, it can't be right. For many Americans, it is the fight that is right, no matter the subject. It is the willingness to fight for a heart-held beliefs that made America as it is today. As Americans became deeply rooted in our newest societies, simply going along for the ride became foreign to us. We need to self-affirm based on these values to be an advocate in a path traveled by someone else. We always want to blaze a new

trail forward, yet will believe in speakers with great vindica-
tion like President Trump and Obama shown in his earlier
Presidential years.

The 60s is when things got provocative:

These years produced anti-war heroes, most of whom you
will know by their names because they became synonymous
with rallying America's youth against multiple governing
Presidencies. The Vietnam War and the Civil Rights movement had their heroes, and each case was different yet similar in procuring commonality within their ranks. The Democratic Party has seen how this worked in the 1960s and led
in most American elections since - when times were good
because of their firm commitment to being one of thought
and action.

*Each of these movements is seen as determinative
events in our society.*

The1960s were revolutionary years for America. It was
stressed with anti-war protests, flag-burning, civil disobedience and assassinations that earmarked this time as our
most decisive recent decade. American's lost their ideals in
the pandemonium, some youth emerged enlightened, but all
of us were affected by the turbulence. We see all this turbulence most in our music compositions of the 60's. The youth
of this era was encircled with the music that became our
culture.

From there to...

Our leaders had to believe they were getting our incredi-
bly burdensome times into order. They believed in being a
higher presence in our lives to help and reconfirm our role
as leaders in the world. We now live in a deeply divided
nation that now faces both challenging domestic issues and
perhaps the most complicated political situation since World
War II. We may be at a point that will determine the fate of
America and the free populist world.

Since the 60's, we've faced ..the worst of society's ills: war, economic upheaval, and social transformation have all seriously kept many in America focused on achieving meaningful transformation.

In our past, leaders such as Presidents Lincoln, Truman, and Eisenhower guided us forward with common sense and pragmatism against governmental over reach. Our best leaders throughout history help strengthen the bonds that unite us as Americans. Many leaders from our past address the broader interests of our country and don't pander to base politics as both parties do today.

America needs a bi-partisan *"Unity"* national policy that should include fixing our decades of failure to create (social) equality all the while building the economy by decreasing inflation. Also, our nation needs to get back to a efficient foreign policy that also bolsters our economic strategy and strengthens our relationships with our worldwide allies. This would include the more effective use of diplomacy, trade and tariffs, that promotes our democratic values to the rest of the world.

Presidents and who made bad decisions:

While evaluations of presidential effectiveness can be subjective and vary based on political beliefs and historical perspectives, several U.S. presidents are often cited by historians and critics as having made decisions that led to negative consequences for the country. Here are a few presidents frequently mentioned in discussions of those who may have made America "worse" in various respects:

1. James Buchanan (1857-1861)
Context: Buchanan served during a time of increasing sectional tension and was unable to effectively address the growing divide between the North and South over slavery.
Consequences: His inaction in the face of rising tensions contributed to the secession of Southern states and the

onset of the Civil War. His belief in not interfering with states' rights and a lack of decisive leadership are often criticized.

2. Andrew Johnson (1865-1869)

Context: Johnson succeeded Abraham Lincoln and oversaw the Reconstruction era following the Civil War.

Consequences: His lenient policies towards the South, opposition to civil rights for freed slaves, and failure to support the Reconstruction Acts led to widespread violence against African Americans and a rollback of many civil rights gains. His presidency is often viewed as a critical failure in advancing racial equality.

3. Warren G. Harding (1921-1923)

Context: Harding's administration was marred by corruption scandals, such as the Teapot Dome scandal, and a general perception of incompetence.

Consequences: The corruption and lack of oversight during his presidency eroded public trust in government and set a precedent for future corruption. His administration is often criticized for a lack of meaningful progress on important issues.

4. Herbert Hoover (1929-1933)

Context: Hoover was president during the onset of the Great Depression.

Consequences: His reliance on voluntary measures and limited government intervention in the economy failed to alleviate the suffering caused by the Depression. His policies were perceived as ineffective, leading to widespread poverty and hardship, which contributed to his electoral defeat in 1932.

5. Richard Nixon (1969-1974)

Context: Nixon's presidency is marked by significant domestic and foreign policy achievements but overshadowed by the Watergate scandal.

Consequences: The scandal led to Nixon's resignation and a significant erosion of public trust in government. The political fallout from Watergate contributed to increased cynicism toward politicians and government institutions.

6. George W. Bush (2001-2009)

Context: Bush's presidency was defined by the events of September 11, 2001, and the subsequent wars in Afghanistan and Iraq.

Consequences: The decision to invade Iraq, based on claims of weapons of mass destruction, led to a prolonged conflict with significant loss of life and regional instability. The protracted nature of the wars, along with the economic downturn in 2008, raised significant concerns about national security, foreign policy, and economic management.

7. Donald Trump (2017-2021)

Context: Trump's presidency was characterized by polarization, contentious rhetoric, and significant policy changes.

Consequences: Critics argue that he exacerbated divisions within the country, undermined democratic norms, and implemented controversial policies regarding immigration, response to climate change, and handling public health issues, particularly during the COVID-19 pandemic. His presidency led to deep political polarization and ongoing debates about governance and accountability.

Assessing the impact of a presidency involves considering various factors, including the context of the times, the challenges faced, and the long-term effects of their policies. While opinions may differ on how much blame to assign to specific presidents for negative outcomes, the leaders mentioned above are frequently included in discussions about the adverse effects of certain presidential administrations on America.

Dems make it worse for America:

The notion that "liberal presidents have destroyed America" reflects a specific critique of the policies and actions of several U.S. presidents typically associated with liberal or progressive ideologies. It's important to note that this viewpoint is subjective and depends on political beliefs, and it can be contentious in nature. Here are several arguments made by critics regarding the impact of certain liberal presidents:

1. Lyndon B. Johnson (1963-1969)

Great Society Programs: Johnson's ambitious Great Society agenda aimed at eliminating poverty and racial injustice through a range of social programs. Critics argue that these programs expanded the welfare state and created dependency on government assistance, undermining personal responsibility and contributing to long-term social issues.

Vietnam War: While Johnson made significant civil rights advancements, his escalation of the Vietnam War led to widespread discontent, protests, and social upheaval, which some argue distracted from domestic priorities and damaged public trust in government.

2. Jimmy Carter (1977-1981)

Economic Challenges: Carter's presidency is often criticized for his management of the economy during a period of stagflation—high inflation paired with unemployment. Critics argue that his policies failed to effectively address these issues, contributing to economic malaise that persisted beyond his presidency.

National Confidence: His speech regarding the "Crisis of Confidence" (often referred to as the "malaise speech") reflected a sense of national discontent that many believe undermined public morale and trust in leadership.

3. Bill Clinton (1993-2001)

Welfare Reform: While Clinton's welfare reform in 1996 aimed to reduce dependency on government assistance, critics claim it negatively affected vulnerable populations and did not adequately address poverty and its root causes.

Economic Inequality: Despite substantial economic growth during his presidency, critics argue that the focus on globalization and free trade (notably NAFTA) contributed to job losses in certain industries and increased economic inequality, hurting working-class Americans.

4. Barack Obama (2009-2017)

Affordable Care Act (Obamacare): While aimed at expanding healthcare access, critics argue that the ACA led to increased healthcare costs for some Americans and created market instability. The rollout faced significant technical issues, which many believe damaged public perception of government efficiency.

Economic Recovery: Although the Obama administration oversaw recovery from the Great Recession, critics contend that the recovery was uneven and did not sufficiently benefit middle-class and lower-income families, exacerbating economic disparities.

5. Joe Biden (2021-present)

Economic Concerns: Early in his presidency, Biden faced significant challenges related to inflation, supply chain issues, and rising gas prices. Critics argue that some of his policies, including massive spending packages aimed at COVID-19 recovery, have contributed to inflationary pressures.

Border and Immigration Issues: Biden's handling of immigration and border security has come under scrutiny, with critics arguing that liberal policies have led to increased numbers of migrants at the southern border and strained resources.

The criticisms of these liberal presidents often center on their economic policies, social programs, and responses to foreign and domestic challenges. Supporters of these presidents would argue that their efforts contributed to significant social progress, civil rights advancements, and improved living standards for many Americans.

Discussions about the impact of liberal presidents on America reflect broader partisan ideologies and highlight the complexities of governance, policymaking, and historical interpretation. Different perspectives contribute to an ongoing debate about the best ways to address the nation's challenges and opportunities.

Chapter One:

A Beginning of Disillusionment:
*Challenges used to make us stronger
as a Nation.*

*Disillusion and apathy might be measured in several ways,
such as low turnout in elections or declining membership of
political parties.*

Our social malaise represents a profound and pervasive
sense of discontent, unease, and dissatisfaction within a society, often stemming from a complex interplay of socioeco-
nomic, political, and cultural factors. Understanding which
United States presidency grappled with the most severe form
of this condition requires a comprehensive analysis of historical periods marked by significant social challenges. This
report will delve into the definition of social malaise within the
American context, examine several presidencies that faced
considerable societal discord, compare these periods based
on key indicators, and ultimately synthesize the findings to
identify the presidency that confronted the most profound
and widespread social malaise.

The first Malaise in my life:
The Great Depression, which my Grandparents lived through
began with the stock market crash of 1929, is often characterized as America's first significant economic malaise that I
can remember, reflecting widespread financial instability, unemployment, and societal despair. It marked a profound turning point in the nation's history, leading to dramatic changes
in government policy, including the New Deal reforms initiated by President Franklin D. Roosevelt. This era not only
highlighted vulnerabilities in the American economic system
but also reshaped the relationship between the government
and the populace, as citizens sought assistance and stability
during a time of unprecedented hardship.

The Great Depression was triggered by a combination of factors, including the 1929 stock market crash, over-speculation in stocks, excessive use of credit, and underlying weaknesses in the banking and agricultural sectors.

Additionally, vulnerabilities such as income inequality, erratic consumer spending, and international financial instability further exacerbated the economic downturn. The collapse of banks and businesses led to massive unemployment and a drastic reduction in consumer spending, creating a vicious cycle that deepened the recession.

Finally, policy responses, including the implementation of tariffs like the Smoot-Hawley Tariff, worsened the situation by stifling international trade. The Smoot-Hawley Tariff, officially known as the Tariff Act of 1930, was enacted in the United States to raise import duties on a wide range of goods in an attempt to protect American industries during the Great Depression.

<u>President Roosevelt created the political monster that is our government.</u>
The **swamp** as it is known today, is a result of un-limited governmental growth and it purposes were changed to be ever-growing and birthing new agencies that were thought to help Americans in need.

- The swamp replicates itself to remain alive and in Power.

The New Deal coalition was an American political coalition that supported the Democratic Party beginning in 1932. The coalition is named after President Franklin D. Roosevelt's New Deal programs, and the follow-up Democratic presidents. It was composed of voting blocs who supported them.

The coalition included labor unions, blue-collar workers, big city machines, racial and religious minorities (especially

Jews, Catholics, and African Americans), white Southerners, and intellectuals.

Besides voters the coalition included powerful interest groups: Democratic Party organizations in most states, city machines, labor unions, some third parties, universities, and foundations.

It was largely opposed by the Republican Party, the business community, and rich Protestants. In creating his coalition, Roosevelt was at first eager to include liberal Republicans and some radical third parties, even if it meant downplaying the "Democratic" name. By the 1940s, the Republican and third-party allies had mostly been defeated.

In 1948, the Democratic Party stood alone and won both the White House and both Congressional houses with a mandate, surviving the splits that created two splinter parties.

The New Deal was a series of programs and projects instituted during the Great Depression by President Franklin D. Roosevelt that aimed to restore prosperity to Americans.

When Roosevelt took office in 1933, he acted swiftly to stabilize the economy and provide jobs and relief to those who were suffering.

Over the next eight years, the government instituted a series of experimental New Deal projects and programs, such as the CCC, the WPA, the TVA, the SEC and others.

Roosevelt's New Deal fundamentally and permanently changed the U.S. federal government by expanding its size and scope—especially its role in the economy.
...and create the swamp of political office bureaucrats that Trump's is trying to change and cut the over spending for us.

- The Emergency Banking
- The First Hundred Days
- Second New Deal
- The End of the New Deal?

The New Deal was a series of programs and projects instituted during the Great Depression by President Franklin D. Roosevelt that aimed to restore prosperity to Americans.

When Roosevelt took office in 1933, he acted swiftly to stabilize the economy and provide jobs and relief to those who were suffering.

Over the next eight years, the government instituted a series of experimental New Deal projects and programs, such as the CCC, the WPA, the TVA, the SEC and others. Roosevelt's New Deal fundamentally and permanently changed the U.S. federal government by expanding its size and scope—especially its role in the economy.

Cost of the New Deal (Adjusted for Inflation):
Initial Spending: The federal government spent about $32 billion between 1933 and 1939. In today's money (adjusted for inflation), this would be around $600 billion to $700 billion.
Post-1939: Roosevelt's administration continued to spend throughout the 1940s, especially as World War II required further government investment. The overall spending during his time in office (1933–1945) is estimated to have exceeded $40 billion—which translates to around $750 billion to $1 trillion in today's dollars.

Key Programs and Costs:
Some of the major programs under the New Deal included:
Civilian Conservation Corps (CCC): About $3 billion ($55 billion adjusted for inflation) was spent to provide jobs for

young men in public works projects like planting trees and building infrastructure.

Works Progress Administration (WPA): Spent around $11 billion ($210 billion adjusted for inflation) creating public works jobs, including roads, schools, and post offices.

Social Security Act: Set up a federal safety net for the elderly and unemployed. The Social Security program's cost is ongoing and has been one of the most expensive federal programs in U.S. history.

Economic Impact:

Short-Term: The immediate effects of the New Deal programs were positive, helping provide jobs, stimulate demand, and stabilize the economy.

Long-Term: The New Deal fundamentally changed the role of the federal government in the American economy, making the government a key player in managing the welfare state and economy, a role that continues today.

Was It Worth It?

The economic cost was enormous, but the long-term benefits—such as Social Security, labor protections, and infrastructure improvements—were profound. Many argue the New Deal was crucial in alleviating the Great Depression, while others debate whether it was the spending or the onset of World War II that truly ended the economic crisis.

Second New Deal:

Despite the best efforts of President Roosevelt and his cabinet, however, the Great Depression continued. Unemployment persisted, the economy remained unstable, farmers continued to struggle in the Dust Bowl and people grew angrier and more desperate.

So, in the spring of 1935, Roosevelt launched a second, more aggressive series of federal programs, sometimes called the Second New Deal.

In April, he created the Works Progress Administration (WPA) to provide jobs for unemployed people. WPA projects weren't allowed to compete with private industry, so they focused on building things like post offices, bridges, schools, highways and parks. The WPA also gave work to artists, writers, theater directors and musicians.

The New Deal coalition created a brand-new, if tenuous, political coalition that included white working people, African Americans and left-wing intellectuals. More women entered the workforce as Roosevelt expanded the number of secretarial roles in government. These groups rarely shared the same interests—at least, they rarely thought they did— but they did share a powerful belief that an interventionist government was good for their families, the economy and the nation.

Sponsored by Senator Reed Smoot and Representative Willis C. Hawley, the tariff aimed to support domestic farmers and manufacturers by making foreign products more expensive. However, it led to retaliatory tariffs from other countries, significantly reducing international trade and exacerbating the economic downturn.

Defining Social Malaise in the American Context:
The concept of social malaise extends beyond individual discontent to describe a collective societal experience of suffering and unease that arises from various underlying socio-economic issues. Historically, the term has evolved from its origins in medical science, where it denotes a general feeling of discomfort or ill-being, to encompass a broader societal condition indicating that a society is perceived to be "not in good health". This societal malaise often manifests as latent feelings of decline, a sense of normelness or anomie, and a lack of trust in political and personal spheres. Within the American context, social malaise can be seen as a consequence of significant societal disruptions that lead to a fragmented and fractioned culture.

The term gained prominence in the late 1970s, particularly in relation to President Jimmy Carter's address to the nation on July 15, 1979. Although Carter himself did not explicitly use the word "malaise," critics soon labeled his speech, which addressed a perceived "crisis of confidence" and an erosion of the nation's will, as the "*malaise speech*". Carter spoke of a growing doubt about the meaning of American lives and a loss of national unity and purpose, suggesting a profound distress where the government seemed no longer to work for a majority of its people. This sentiment resonated with the concept of "middle-class malaise" that emerged during the late 1970s, characterized by disillusionment, anxiety, and dissatisfaction among middle-class Americans due to economic turmoil, including high inflation and energy crises.

Social unrest serves as a critical indicator of social malaise, representing the collective dissatisfaction and actions of a group or society against perceived injustices and inequalities within the social system. This can manifest in various forms, such as protests, strikes, riots, and other acts of civil disobedience. The sociological concept of anomie, referring to a state where societal norms are unclear or have eroded, is also useful in understanding social malaise. Anomie can lead to feelings of self-centeredness, a reduction in altruism and compassion, distrust of others, apathy, alienation, and anger, all contributing to a sense of societal ill-being.

Key indicators of social malaise in the American context include social unrest, economic hardship, cultural divisions, and public dissatisfaction. These factors are often interconnected; for instance, economic hardship can fuel social unrest and exacerbate cultural divisions, while a lack of public trust can undermine efforts to address any of these issues. Therefore, a comprehensive assessment of social malaise requires examining the presence and severity of these interconnected indicators.

A Historical Survey of American Presidencies and Social Challenges.

Throughout United States history, several presidencies have been marked by significant social issues that could be indicative of social malaise. While early presidencies faced monumental challenges such as the Civil War and Reconstruction, this analysis will focus on the 20th and early 21st centuries, drawing upon the provided research material.

Major Social Challenges Faced by American Presidents during the 20th Century

Civil rights and racial disparities:
Presidents ranging from Theodore Roosevelt to Lyndon B. Johnson faced persistent racial discrimination and segregation, particularly in the South. The civil rights movement of the 1950s and 1960s compelled presidents such as Kennedy and Johnson to address legal and social disparities, culminating in landmark legislation like the Civil Rights Act and Voting Rights

Economic crises.
Franklin D. Roosevelt's defining challenge was the Great Depression, which caused widespread unemployment and poverty. His New Deal programs sought to provide relief, recovery, and reform, but benefits were not evenly distributed, and many minorities remained disadvantaged.

After World War II, Harry Truman was tasked with transitioning the economy from wartime to peacetime, dealing with inflation, labor strikes, and reintegrating millions of veterans into civilian life.

Workplace Unrest:
Labor strikes and union demands were major issues, particularly after WWII. Presidents had to strike a balance between

workers' rights and economic stability, as demonstrated by Truman's struggles with strikes and the passage of the Taft-Hartley Act.

Enhancement of Presidential Authority and Public Trust:
The expansion of executive authority, the use of executive orders, and the growing complexity of the federal bureaucracy posed new challenges. Presidents had to navigate disagreements with Congress over war powers, budgets, and the limits of executive action, particularly after Watergate and the Vietnam War1.

Information and Media:
By the late twentieth century, presidents were confronted with untrustworthy information sources, skewed public opinion polls, and the power of special interest groups, all exacerbated by the rise of television and political advertising.

Social Movements and Public Pressure
Grassroots activism, whether for civil rights, labor, or other causes, has frequently forced presidents to respond to social demands rather than initiating change.
These challenges forced presidents to adapt their leadership, often in the face of intense public scrutiny and political opposition, thereby shaping the evolution of the presidency and American society throughout the century.

5 reasons for generational disillusionment

Generational disillusionment is a complex issue that affects every cohort, from Baby Boomers to Generation Alpha. Each generation has faced unique challenges and socio-political contexts that have shaped their world views and left them feeling disillusioned in different ways. In this context, disillusionment refers to a profound sense of disappointment or disconnection from the expectations, dreams, and ideals that influenced their formative years. This disillusionment may arise from factors such as broken promises of prosperity, unmet emotional needs, or the challenges posed by a hyper-digital age. Ultimately, generational disillusionment influences how each group interacts with the world. Let's explore the reasons behind the disillusionment experienced by each generation.

Generational disillusionment is a complex issue that affects every cohort, from Baby Boomers to Generation Alpha. Each generation has faced unique challenges and sociopolitical contexts that have shaped their worldviews and left them feeling disillusioned in different ways. In this context, disillusionment refers to a profound sense of disappointment or disconnection from the expectations, dreams, and ideals that influenced their formative years. This disillusionment may arise from factors such as broken promises of prosperity, unmet emotional needs, or the challenges posed by a hyper-digital age.

Ultimately, generational disillusionment influences how each group interacts with the world. Let's explore the reasons behind the disillusionment experienced by each generation.

Baby Boomers: The material dream (having more stuff then your parents) that didn't deliver What many promised.

The **Baby Boomer** generation, born between 1946 and 1964, came of age during one of the most prosperous periods in American history. They grew up in a time characterized by post-World War II economic expansion, the rise of suburbia, and the emergence of the American Dream, which promised a life filled with material wealth and success. This generation experienced significant social and political changes, including the civil rights movement and the Vietnam War, all set against a backdrop of increasing consumerism and greater access to higher education.

However, despite this apparent success, many Baby Boomers have become disillusioned as they enter their retirement years. Their disappointment stems from discovering that the material benefits they worked so hard for — homes, cars, and career advancement — didn't fulfill their expectations.

While they were told that financial stability and material accumulation would lead to happiness, many found that their pursuit of the "American Dream" left them empty and unfulfilled because they hadn't "kept up" with the Jones" as everyone had to accomplish to feel successful.

Those who sought meaning through faith and spiritual pursuits often found lasting satisfaction that transcended their material success. In contrast, those who placed all their hope in material gain have become cynical, realizing too late that money, possessions, and status were never enough to meet their innermost desires.

Generation X: The emotional disconnect of the latchkey generation that made some great decisions by themselves without parental malaise or guidance.

Generation X, born between 1965 and 1980, is often called the "latchkey generation." This is because many Gen Xers grew up with two working parents or in single-parent households, meaning they often returned home from school to an empty house. Their independence, resilience, and adaptability were shaped by these experiences and by witnessing significant cultural shifts, including the rise of personal computing and the end of the Cold War.

Despite their ability to adapt to a rapidly changing world, Generation X has faced deep disillusionment, largely due to the emotional disconnect they experienced growing up. Many Gen Xers grew up in households where their parents were focused on hard work and career advancement, leaving little time for emotional connection. While their parents may have provided materially, the lack of emotional investment left many Gen Xers feeling abandoned and disconnected.

This generational gap created a profound sense of disillusionment. Many in Generation X feel they missed out on the emotional nurturing they needed during their formative years, leading to skepticism toward institutions like family, church, and work.

Millennials: Disillusioned by the unattainable American Dream

Millennials, born between 1981 and 1996, grew up during the rise of the internet and digital technology. They came of age during the early 2000s, when the promises of success and prosperity were still heavily touted. However, the economic realities of adulthood did not align with the optimistic picture painted for them in their youth. Many Millennials entered the workforce during or after the Great Recession, facing stagnant wages, skyrocketing student loan debt, and an increasingly unaffordable housing market.

Their disillusionment stems from their inability to achieve the same financial success and stability as previous generations. The "American Dream" of homeownership, financial independence, and upward mobility has become elusive for many Millennials. The cost of living has outpaced wage growth, making it difficult for them to buy homes or start families, even with college degrees and full-time jobs.

This economic hardship has led many Millennials to question the systems and structures that were supposed to provide them with opportunity. Many feel that they have been dealt a bad hand and have grown cynical toward traditional institutions like the government, the financial system, and even, in some cases, organized religion, which they feel have failed to deliver on their promises.

Generation Z: Cynicism toward institutions

Generation Z, born between 1997 and 2012, is the first generation to grow up entirely in the digital age. They are tech-savvy, diverse, and socially conscious, with strong opinions on climate change, social justice, and political reform. However, their disillusionment is rooted in the education and societal systems that have taught them to be cynical toward traditional institutions, including churches, the U.S. government, and older generations.

Gen Z, the Most Pessimistic Generation in History.
More young people today say they find it difficult to have hope for the world than at any time since 1976.

Roughly 41 million Generation Z Americans—ages 18 to 27. Generation Z is among the most liberal segments of the electorate.

According to long-running interviews with dozens of young people across the country, young adults in Generation Z (those born in 1997 or later) emerged from the pandemic feeling more disillusioned than any previous generation. They are concerned that they will never earn enough money to achieve the same level of security as previous generations, citing a delayed transition into adulthood, an impenetrable housing market, and a mountain of student debt.

And, they are tired of policymakers from both parties. Gen Z's widespread gloom is manifesting in unprecedented skepticism of Washington and despair that either party's leaders can help. Young Americans' entire political memories are consumed by intense partisanship and warnings about the impending demise of everything from US democracy to the planet.

Dissatisfaction is driving some young voters to third-party candidates in this year's presidential race, while others are considering staying home on Election Day or leaving the top of the ballot blank. While young people typically vote at lower rates, a small number of Generation Z voters could swing the election, which was decided four years ago by tens of thousands of votes in several swing states.

> *Confidence:* When asked if they trusted various public institutions, Gen Z's confidence was generally lower than that of older cohorts at the same age.

Only one-third of Generation Z Americans identify as conservative and there is now a higher proportion of conservatives than when millennials, Generation X, and baby boomers took the survey at the same age, though some of the differences were minor and within the surveys margin of error.

According to a University of Michigan survey that has tracked public sentiment among 12th-graders for nearly five decades, more young people now say they have lost hope in the world than at any time since at least 1976.

Generation Z's future outcomes:
As a result of the global pandemic, Generation Z has spent years in chronic isolation, a lack of social interaction, and a proclivity to spend excessive amounts of time online.

Economic Reality:
Gen Z may be the first generation in US history to be less fortunate than their parents. Many people have given up on ever being able to afford a home.

The economy is supposedly booming. Regardless, debt-related stress is high among younger millennials and zoomers.

Everything is great.:
When you add it all up, everything looks pretty good. This is why we have seen so many stories attempting to explain why people should be happy.

However, Biden's problems are not solely due to his partisanship. If that were the case, Biden would not be polling so poorly among Democrats in general, blacks, and young people. Okay, there is some partisanship in the polls.

Inflation plus recession equals stagflation.

Election's Impact:
If No Labels ever gets its act together, I believe it will sway more votes from Biden than Trump. Many people, however, will simply sit it out. Young voters in 2020 were encouraged to vote against Trump. Now they have given up.

Many Gen Zers have been exposed to critical narratives about the failures of previous generations, especially concerning issues like racism, inequality, and environmental destruction.

They have grown up in a world constantly bombarded with negative news, political division, and economic instability. This has fostered a deep cynicism toward the established order, with many feeling disconnected from the values and practices of previous generations. However, with the rise of societal fragmentation, many have sought a more traditional way of life and have become more conservative in their values than the previous generation.

Generation Alpha:
Disconnected in a technological world

Generation Alpha, born from 2013 onward, is the first to be raised entirely in the age of smartphones, artificial intelligence, and digital integration. While this generation is still young, early signs of disillusionment and emotional detachment are already emerging. Their disillusionment is rooted in the disconnect from being raised in a hyper-digital world where social media, video games, and virtual reality dominate their interactions.

While Generation Alpha is more technologically immersed than any previous generation, they are also more isolated regarding physical relationships and real-world experiences. Many are growing up with less face-to-face interaction, spending more time on screens than with peers or family members. This constant digital consumption and the rise of artificial intelligence may make them feel increasingly disconnected from real human relationships and communities. Their challenge will be to navigate a world where technology enhances their lives without leaving them emotionally and spiritually empty.

Generational disillusionment is a widespread phenomenon that has impacted every age group.

From Baby Boomers discovering that material wealth cannot bring fulfillment to Generation Alpha facing the emotional vacuum of a hyper-digital world, each generation has unique struggles. However, the common thread in all these experiences is the need for deeper meaning and connection — something that can only be found in faith, community, and a relationship with God. As each generation grapples with its disillusionment, the Church must rise to meet these needs by offering hope, purpose, and a path to genuine fulfillment that transcends the fleeting promises of the world.

Presidents make the biggest differences:

Key presidencies to consider include that of Herbert Hoover during the Great Depression, Lyndon B. Johnson during the 1960s with the Civil Rights Movement and the Vietnam War, Jimmy Carter in the late 1970s facing stagflation and an energy crisis , Richard Nixon during the Watergate era, and Donald Trump (2017-2021) amidst significant political polarization and social unrest.

Carter plays upon Nixon's weakness.

Jimmy Carter's presidential campaign in 1976 effectively capitalized on the perceived weaknesses of Richard Nixon, particularly the fallout from the Watergate scandal and broader public disillusionment with government. Here are some key ways Carter played upon Nixon's weaknesses:

Trust and Integrity:

Public Disillusionment: The Watergate scandal severely damaged public trust in the presidency and government institutions. Carter's image as an outsider and a moral leader resonated with voters seeking transparency and honesty in government. He emphasized his integrity, contrasting his clean image with Nixon's controversial reputation.

- "I Will Never Lie to You": Carter's campaign slogan reinforced his commitment to honesty and ethical leadership, appealing to a populace wary of political deceit.

Outsider Status:

Rejection of Establishment Politics: Carter positioned himself as a political outsider and reformer. By doing so, he distanced himself from Nixon's administration, which was associated with the establishment and the political elite. This outsider status helped him attract voters who were disillusioned with traditional politics.

- Connecting with "Everyday Americans": Carter focused on grassroots campaigning, emphasizing his roots in Georgia and his experience as a peanut farmer, which helped him connect with average Americans and present himself as a candidate who understood their concerns.

Focus on Domestic Issues:

Economic Concerns: During Nixon's presidency, the economy faced significant turmoil, including inflation and unemployment. Carter capitalized on these issues by presenting himself as a candidate capable of addressing economic challenges through innovative policies and focusing on energy conservation and alternative energy sources, distinguishing himself from Nixon's administration.

Social Issues: Carter took a compassionate stance on social issues, promoting civil rights and social justice initiatives, which resonated well with voters who were concerned about Nixon's legacy and the lack of focus on these issues during his administration.

Restoration of Democracy:

Promise to Restore Democratic Values: Carter campaigned on the idea of restoring ethical governance and democratic principles. He presented himself as a unifier who would heal the divisions caused by Nixon's presidency and the scandals that followed, appealing to voters' desire for change.

Vietnam and Foreign Policy:

Critique of Nixon's Foreign Policy: While Nixon was credited with opening relations with China and pursuing détente with the Soviet Union, his foreign policy was also viewed critically, especially in the context of Vietnam. Carter emphasized a more humane foreign policy approach, focusing on human rights and ethical considerations in international relations.

Outcome:

Carter's ability to effectively frame his candidacy in contrast to Nixon's weaknesses played a crucial role in his electoral success in 1976. By promoting a message of integrity, healing, and responsiveness to the American people's needs,

Carter was able to resonate with voters who were disillusioned by the events of the early 1970s.

The fact that these presidencies span different decades underscores that social malaise is not unique to any single period but can manifest in various ways depending on the prevailing historical, economic, and political circumstances.

Deep Dive into Periods of Significant Social Malaise.

The Hoover Presidency (*The Great Depression*)

The presidency of Herbert Hoover, from 1929 to 1933, coincided with the most severe economic downturn in United States history, the Great Depression. Following the stock market crash of October 1929, the nation plunged into a period of economic collapse characterized by a dramatic rise in unemployment, which reached nearly 25% by 1933. Hoover initially underestimated the severity of the crisis and his administration's efforts to mitigate the economic devastation were largely seen as inadequate. Widespread poverty, business failures, and bank closings became commonplace. This economic hardship fueled significant social unrest, including hunger marches, small riots, and the poignant Bonus Army protest where World War I veterans demanded early payment of their promised bonuses. The era also saw increases in crime rates, suicide rates, and malnutrition, reflecting the desperation and hopelessness felt by many Americans. A profound loss of faith in the government's ability to resolve the crisis permeated the nation. The sheer scale of economic devastation during the Great Depression, affecting nearly all aspects of life and leading to widespread destitution and a breakdown of social order, represents a profound level of social malaise.

The Johnson Presidency (The 1960s)

The 1960s under President Lyndon B. Johnson were a period of immense social upheaval and transformation. The Civil Rights Movement gained significant momentum, challenging deeply entrenched racial segregation and discrimination, often met with violent resistance. This era also witnessed widespread urban riots, often referred to as "ghetto riots," fueled by persistent racial inequality and instances of police brutality.

The 1960s under President Johnson were indeed a time of profound social upheaval, marked by both significant progress and intense conflict. The Civil Rights Movement's push for equality and justice directly confronted long-standing systemic racism, leading to landmark legislation but also sparking fierce and often violent resistance from those invested in maintaining the existing racial hierarchy.

The Urban riots, frequently referred to as "ghetto riots," were another stark manifestation of the deep-seated racial inequalities and frustrations that simmered beneath the surface of American society. These events, often triggered by specific incidents of perceived injustice, laid bare the consequences of decades of segregation, discrimination, and economic marginalization in urban centers.

It's important to remember that these two phenomena – the Civil Rights Movement and the urban riots – while distinct in their methods and goals, were interconnected. Both stemmed from the pervasive issue of racial inequality in America, albeit expressed in different ways. The Civil Rights Movement sought to dismantle discriminatory laws and practices through nonviolent direct action and legal challenges, while the urban riots often erupted as expressions of rage and despair in response to systemic oppression and lack of opportunity.

These riots resulted in significant loss of life, injuries, numerous arrests, and extensive property damage. Simultaneously, the escalation of the Vietnam War led to increasing American casualties, sparking widespread anti-war protests and creating deep and bitter divisions within American society. Public opinion increasingly turned against the war, further fracturing the nation. The decade was also marked by significant cultural upheaval and social change, including the rise of the counterculture movement. The assassinations of key figures like President John F. Kennedy and Martin Luther King Jr. further contributed to a pervasive sense of instability by intense social and political polarization driven by the struggle for civil rights and the divisive Vietnam War, leading to widespread social unrest and a deep societal crisis.

Counterculture: The emergence of the counterculture, symbolized by the hippie movement and events like the Woodstock Festival (1969), represented a rejection of mainstream societal norms and values. This movement often criticized the consumerism, materialism, and conformity of the post-World War II era, leading to conflicts with more traditional social structures.

Youth Discontent: A general disillusionment among youth was palpable during this decade, driven by changing cultural norms, a desire for greater freedom, and a rejection of authoritarianism. This youth culture often felt alienated from mainstream institutions and expressed dissatisfaction through art, music, and activism.

Generational Divide: The 1960s were marked by stark generational divides, with older and younger generations often clashing over issues of war, civil rights, and cultural values. This divide contributed to a sense of societal fragmentation and malaise.

The Carter Presidency (The Late 1970s)

President Jimmy Carter's term in office, from 1977 to 1981, was largely defined by a unique and challenging economic situation known as stagflation – a combination of high inflation, stagnant economic growth, and high unemployment. The nation also faced a severe energy crisis, marked by rapidly rising oil prices and shortages. Beyond these economic woes, there was a palpable sense of a "crisis of confidence" among the American people, a feeling of lost national unity and purpose. Public trust in the government's ability to effectively address these mounting problems eroded significantly. Additionally, rising crime rates and the deterioration of inner cities contributed to the overall sense of malaise. While the Carter years did not experience the same level of violent social unrest as the 1960s, the pervasive sense of economic anxiety and national decline significantly impacted the national psyche, fostering a deep social malaise.

He declared the "Carter Doctrine," warning the Soviets that he would protect U.S. interests in the Middle East "by force if necessary." And he ordered the establishment of a rapid deployment force, which would be capable of delivering a massive U.S. military capability into the Persian Gulf.

Carter won the presidency in 1976 with the support of organized labor and with the Democratic Party having pledged support for a number of significant progressive policies, including the creation of a federal Consumer Protection Agency, union-friendly labor law reform, and legislation mandating that the government ensure full employment. But the president and the Democratic-controlled Congress ended up initiating the turn toward anti-worker neo-liberalism that Carter's successors in both parties would carry out for the next four decades.

Despite Democrats' super-majority, legislation for the Consumer Protection Agency and increased penalties for unfair labor practices failed in Congress due to organized business opposition. Congress did eventually pass, and Carter signed, the Humphrey-Hawkins Full Employment and Balanced Growth Act of 1978 — but only after it had been watered down to a merely symbolic measure, stripping out language that would have required the government to ensure full employment and create public jobs when private sector hiring fell short.

Carter so eloquently bemoaned to metastasize, you could do worse than enacting the very policies his own administration implemented: cutting taxes, shrinking the welfare state, de-regulating the economy, and turning away from the increas-ingly besieged labor movement. These measures paved the way for a few at the top to grow fabulously wealthy, while the majority of Americans saw their wages stagnate and their unions destroyed while suffering the consequences of the ul-trarich's reckless, self-serving decisions. Our Second Gilded Age of obscene inequality and atomization is the predictable result of such policies.

Jimmy Carter rightly warned against the country taking a path that would lead to "fragmentation and self-interest. Down that road lies a mistaken idea of freedom, the right to grasp for ourselves some advantage over others. That path would be one of constant conflict between narrow interests ending in chaos and immobility." It is a bit of tragic irony that he helped lead us further down that road.

In hindsight, Carter's speech was startlingly prescient. The unchecked consumerism he lamented has metastasized into a culture of debt, environmental degradation, and social fragmentation. His plea for energy independence remains as urgent as ever in the face of climate change and the geopo-litical instability tied to fossil fuel dependence. Carter warned us, with clarity that grows sharper in retrospect, that ignoring these challenges would exact a heavy toll.

"To maintain the buying power that $100 had on the month Carter was sworn into office, you'd need $150 by the time he left the White House just four years later."

The Nixon Presidency (The Watergate Era)
The presidency of Richard Nixon, particularly during the Wa-tergate era (1972-1974), was marked by a profound political crisis that deeply affected American society. The Watergate

scandal, stemming from a break-in at the Democratic National Committee headquarters and the subsequent cover-up by the Nixon administration, led to a major erosion of public trust in the government and political institutions. In fact, polling data suggests that trust in government was lower after Watergate than it is in more recent times. The scandal exacerbated existing political polarization and social divisions within the country. While Nixon also grappled with economic issues, including inflation, the defining characteristic of his presidency in terms of social malaise was the deep crisis of trust it engendered. The revelations of government misconduct at the highest levels created a lasting sense of societal unease and cynicism.

You're right to highlight the profound impact of the Nixon presidency and the Watergate scandal on American society. It undeniably created a deep and lasting scar on public trust in government. The details you provide about the break-in, the cover-up, and the resulting erosion of trust paint a clear picture of this pivotal moment in American political history.

While the economic challenges of inflation during Nixon's presidency were significant and contributed to the overall sense of unease, the Watergate scandal struck at the very heart of the relationship between the government and the people. It wasn't just about economic hardship; it was about a perceived betrayal of trust and a deliberate undermining of democratic principles.

The revelations of abuse of power, obstruction of justice, and a culture of secrecy emanating from the highest levels of government fostered a deep-seated suspicion that extended beyond Nixon himself. It cast a shadow over the integrity of political institutions and fueled a more general questioning of governmental authority.

This erosion of trust has had a lasting impact on American political discourse. We continue to see echoes of this suspicion in public attitudes towards government, the media, and political figures. The Watergate era arguably contributed to a more cynical and polarized political landscape, where questioning motives and uncovering potential wrongdoing became more central to the publics engagement with politics.

Therefore, while economic anxieties certainly contribute to social malaise, the unique nature of the Watergate scandal – a direct assault on the foundations of democratic governance and public trust – makes it a defining characteristic of that era's social unease, with consequences that continue to shape our political reality today.

The comparison to current levels of trust, with polling data suggesting lower trust after Watergate, is a powerful indicator of the scandal's severity and lasting consequences. It underscores how deeply shaken the public was by the revelations of misconduct at the highest levels of power.

Beyond the immediate political ramifications, the Watergate era also significantly contributed to the increasing political polarization and social divisions you mentioned. The scandal exposed a level of partisan conflict and governmental abuse that likely fueled cynicism and made it harder for people with differing political views to find common ground.

While Nixon's presidency also dealt with significant economic challenges like inflation, it's accurate to say that the crisis of trust stemming from Watergate became the defining characteristic of that era's social malaise. The scandal left a legacy of suspicion and questioning of governmental authority that continues to resonate in American political discourse.

Is there anything specific you'd like to discuss further about the Watergate era and its impact? Perhaps we could explore the specific ways in which trust was eroded, the long-term consequences for political institutions, or the connections between Watergate and subsequent periods of political polarization.

The Trump Presidency (2017-2021)

The presidency of Donald Trump, from 2017 to 2021, was characterized by a high volume of sustained protests across the United States, addressing a wide array of grievances including racial injustice, immigration policies, and responses to the COVID-19 pandemic. These protests often exhibited a broad geographic spread. The Trump era was also marked by a significant increase in political polarization and social divisions, with heightened tensions and distrust evident between different segments of the population. This period saw a rise in right-wing counter mobilization and far-right activity.

Furthermore, there were notable challenges to democratic institutions and norms, particularly surrounding claims of election fraud, which culminated in the January 6th. While the economy experienced mixed performance during this time , the persistent and widespread social unrest, coupled with deep political and social divisions, suggests a significant degree of social malaise.

Comparative Analysis: Measuring the Depth and Breadth of Social Malaise

Comparing the scale and impact of social issues across these presidencies reveals distinct patterns. The Great Depression under Hoover had the most devastating economic impact, plunging a vast majority of Americans into poverty and unemployment. The 1960s under Johnson witnessed the most intense and widespread social unrest in terms of violent urban riots and massive anti-war demonstrations, resulting in significant loss of life and property. The Carter years were characterized by a unique combination of economic stagnation and a pervasive sense of national malaise, fueled by stagflation and an energy crisis. The Nixon presidency was defined by a profound crisis of trust in government stemming from the Watergate scandal. The Trump presidency saw a high volume of sustained protests and significant political polarization across numerous social and political issues.

The duration of these periods of malaise also varied. The Great Depression persisted for over a decade, leaving a lasting scar on American society. The intense social unrest of the 1960s spanned several years, coinciding with the peak of the Civil Rights Movement and the escalation of the Vietnam War. The economic difficulties and sense of malaise during the Carter years lasted for his entire term. The Watergate scandal unfolded over approximately two years, but its impact on public trust was long-lasting. The high levels of protest and polarization under Trump were sustained throughout his presidency.

Evaluating the government's response to these challenges provides further context. Hoover's initial response to the Depression was widely criticized as inadequate. Johnson's administration achieved landmark civil rights legislation but struggled to manage the escalating Vietnam War and the widespread urban unrest. Carter's efforts to combat stagflation were largely unsuccessful and may have contributed to the prevailing sense of malaise. Nixon's administration's attempts to cover up the Watergate scandal only deepened the crisis of trust. Trump's often confrontational rhetoric towards protests may have exacerbated social divisions. The effectiveness of the government's response appears to be a critical factor in either mitigating or amplifying social malaise. Periods where governmental actions were perceived as insufficient or contributing to the problems often saw a deepening of societal discontent.

Diverse Perspectives on Social Malaise

It is crucial to acknowledge that the assessment of social malaise is inherently subjective and can vary significantly depending on individual experiences, perspectives, and values. For example, Carter's "malaise" speech was interpreted by some as an attempt to blame the American public for the nation's problems. The Civil Rights Movement, while striving for equality and justice, was met with fierce resistance and viewed very differently by those who benefited from the existing social order. Similarly, the protests against President Trump were seen by some as legitimate expressions of concern over his policies and actions, while others viewed them as unwarranted opposition. Understanding these diverse perspectives is essential for a nuanced appreciation of the complexities of social malaise during different historical periods. What one segment of the population perceives as a period of crisis and decline, another might experience as a time of necessary change or even progress.

Synthesizing the Findings: Identifying the Presidency with the Worst Social Malaise.

Based on the comparative analysis of the key indicators of social malaise – economic hardship, social unrest, cultural divisions, and public dissatisfaction – the presidency of Herbert Hoover during the Great Depression arguably confronted the most widespread and severe social malaise in United States history. The sheer scale of the economic collapse during this period had a profound and devastating impact on nearly every facet of American life, leading to mass unemployment, widespread poverty, and a pervasive sense of despair. While the 1960s under President Johnson witnessed intense social unrest and deep cultural divisions, the fundamental economic fabric of society remained largely intact compared to the Depression era. The malaise experienced during the Carter years, though significant, did not reach the same levels of destitution and widespread economic collapse. The crises of trust under Nixon and the political polarization under Trump were profound and had lasting consequences, but their immediate impact on the daily lives of a majority of Americans may have been less encompassing than the economic catastrophe of the 1930s. Therefore, considering the interconnectedness and severity of economic hardship, social unrest fueled by economic desperation, and the widespread public despair, the Great Depression under Hoover represents the period of the most profound social malaise.

The Legacy of Social Malaise under Herbert Hoover

The presidency of Herbert Hoover faced a period of unparalleled social malaise, primarily driven by the catastrophic economic collapse of the Great Depression. This era was characterized by mass unemployment, widespread poverty, and a profound loss of hope for millions of Americans. The social unrest of the time, including hunger marches and protests, reflected the desperation and suffering endured by a significant portion of the population. The long-term consequences of this period were transformative, leading to a fundamental shift in the role of government in American society, the establishment of crucial social safety nets, and a lasting impact on the national consciousness regarding economic security. The experience of the Great Depression serves as a stark reminder of the fragility of economic prosperity and the potential for widespread social malaise when basic economic needs are unmet. It also underscores the critical role of government intervention and effective leadership in times of profound national crisis.

You've accurately captured the profound social malaise that defined Herbert Hoover's presidency during the Great Depression. The scale of human suffering – the mass unemployment, the pervasive poverty – created a deep sense of despair and a fundamental questioning of the existing social and economic order.

The hunger marches and protests you mentioned were powerful manifestations of this desperation. They weren't just about a lack of resources; they represented a breakdown of faith in the system's ability to provide basic necessities and a growing sense of injustice.

It's crucial to emphasize the transformative long-term consequences of this period. The Great Depression served as a crucible, forging a new understanding of the government's role in American life. The establishment of social safety nets under subsequent administrations, like Social Security and unemployment insurance, directly stemmed from the perceived failures of the Hoover administration's more laissez-faire approach. This era permanently altered the national consciousness regarding economic security, embedding the idea that society, through its government, had a responsibility to protect its most vulnerable members.

The stark reminder of economic fragility and the necessity of effective leadership during crises are indeed key legacies of the Hoover years. The experience of the Great Depression continues to inform policy debates about economic regulation, social welfare, and the appropriate governmental response to economic downturns. It stands as a powerful historical lesson about the human cost of widespread economic hardship and the potential for profound social malaise when basic needs are unmet.

Are there any particular aspects of the social malaise under Hoover that you'd like to explore further? Perhaps we could discuss the specific social unrest movements, the psychological impact of the Depression on individuals and families, or the evolution of political thought in response to this crisis.

It turns out that even our founding fathers had misgivings about their new American Constitution. President Washington was a *Head of State* who saw the scraps and squabbles between Congress and his Cabinet as a serious dismantling and the dividing of the newly formed American United States.

We have as of late taken for granted that elections were candid and legitimate. It has been suggested in recent national elections that this might be false. This and other issues have germinated a serious distrust in our American leadership.

Elections of the recent decades have proven to be of great importance in our population's perception of correctness. The landslide of President Nixon was determined because he was righteously fighting another candidate with utterly, at the time, UN-American values. President Reagan was voted in because Carter told us to embrace failure as a mantra for the new American way of life. Reagan's vision of America was highly elevated more than what President Carter told us in his Malaise speech, which said we should be happy with falling American norms. Reagan led off his campaign against stagflation and a military led by weak politicians with the quip: "A recession is when your neighbor loses his job. A depression is when you lose yours, and a recovery is when Jimmy Carter loses his." Carter's mantra was that we should just get used to being crapped all over by oil producing nations, and that led to a 55% increase in oil prices in the spring of 1979. The USSR was retaining and detaining us passively in different parts of the world and the economy was the only thing that we were looking forward to was record level 12% inflation that introduced Americans to something called *stagflation*. President Reagan curbed the USSR with our economic strength and renewed American military strength, that would not be throttled by mediocre and spineless politicians. Like President Kennedy, Reagan's vision was that Americans could do anything, and this led all of us out of the Carter years' Malaise.

Most of the issues that we will discuss in these pages will be in part because of what I have experienced, and partially how I see events from a disengaged posture.

In 2021, seven percent of American youth 18 to 29 thought America was on the right course and would continue to prosper.

I have been actively looking for the whys and how's this got so bad. Now our Nation's point of view is indifference because we know nothing is going to change for the better with our elected legislature. In the past years, Americans have been asked before elections what they think about the next five years ahead of them. Since President Carter's years in office, it has been said that polled Americans are not looking forward to their future. This is how our malaise continues today. But why?

President Carter had to place a 55 mph speed limit on our highways to save gas nationwide - that truly hurt Americans in their daily lives, because the Saudi's wanted to break the great Western devil. This year there isn't a gasoline shortage from overseas, yet prices are much higher than in previous years. In my opinion, it is because we could be harvesting oil from lands the Government controls, but we don't. It is regulations and self-inflicted policies that made these inflationary events raise the prices of gasoline by 300%. As working class Americans see their paychecks dwindle because their fuel costs getting to and from work to earn that salary, has risen so much in a short period of time.

President Carter also told Americans to lower their heaters to 65 degrees to save heating oil fuel yet, Americans are now being told Natural gas and Clean Coal should be abandoned because they aren't good for our planet. The government says Americans should instead use electricity. The problem with this is that electric grids can be manipulated via hackers or, our government adding usage restrictions. We see this happening in California, our local governments are limiting electric usage to cool homes because they need the power for other critical parts of the electric grid. What happens when electric cars are mandatory in big cities and the grids can't meet the needs of all the extra drain on the system? Or a hacker affects parts of the grid and overloads the rest of the system.

Future Goals vs. Reality.

We as Americans are failed by our leadership. We fail at future-related goals the most. Look at Social Security. Our leaders have been robbing that war chest for years. They call it borrowing, but we know we have to borrow from the Chinese to replenish it every year.

Going to space can be the best example. This experiment cost at today's dollar value $225 billion dollars on a program that has been used very little after a few accomplishments. Without Russia pushing us, America probably would not have been interested in this record shattering program. After we reached the moon, the program fell into disrepair. The next endeavor was to create a space station and a craft that could be used multiple times returning from space to earth. What did this program give us for the last few decades?

After spacecraft Challenger had blown up under the Carter Administration, our people no longer looked with optimism toward traveling to the Moon as did President Kennedy. Kennedy used this win for his administration, which was mired in other failed operations. Unfortunately President Nixon took all the credit for the moon landing because it happened on his watch. The space program did pave the way towards satellite launches and gaining larger rocketry for nuclear bombs. Today we have had most successes hidden from view. I think success in space was too scary for us because it meant we could not be the only ones traveling from planet to planet.

Even though the U.S. government has admitted recently there are Aliens from other planets visiting us, we are continuously overlooking what will happen in that future scenario. Is our future reality planned, or is it an accident? The realities of the past suggest that Presidential policies are reactive only dealing with outcomes rather than proactive planning to help harness future events.

President Washington in his farewell address covered everything we face today. Hyper partisanship, inner fighting between Cabinet members and Congress, interference of elections and the fear of excess debt were earmarked in that speech. So if 200 years ago we knew what to look to prevent, why are we doing exactly what he warned us not to do? Is it that we can not learn from previous experiences, like you do as you grow from childhood to adulthood?

Abraham Lincoln used Washington's wisdom. He quoted Washington on some of the same things that happened 100 years earlier. As Lincoln started a new party, called the Republicans, it was Washington's experience and words of wisdom that taught Lincoln how to deal with starting a new party. As the Southern Democrats organized the war between the States, Lincoln recalled Washington's speech and gave the speech word for word to the Union Army in the opening hours of the Civil War. Lincoln pronounced himself as Washington's heir, just as modern day Republicans say about being Lincoln's heir.

Another great yet short-lived Presidency was Eisenhower's. Being part of the military machine that grew in strength during this commander's status in the US armed services, and then serving in politics, taught him to be careful being a part of the new military machine - that he used so successfully. President Eisenhower cautioned us like, he could see the future that had actually come true. He told us to fear the men who held and controlled military power. Ultimate power breeds contentment in holding, welding and having control of others through this potential. Men controlling the world's ultimate military power is what he was warning us about. It is human nature to abuse this competence. It is in part why our Bill of Rights were authored to regulate the kingly powers given to the faction who run our government. So two of our white knight military Generals warned us about the military -industrial complex but here we are, war after war, making the military and their suppliers filthy rich.

Predominantly, many Presidents warn about America's fiscal policies. Eisenhower divulge generational responsibility many times. He stated over and over we should not burden our children and their children with our obtuse debt. Many Americans think we should listen to people with this author- itative and insightful view of what could be next in American society.

Previous presidents have told us of what can help the mod- ern world's peoples from a speech written 200 years before. An inspiring speech given by President Reagan at Moscow university told of a time when American and U.S.S.R.'s peoples could eliminate the threat of nuclear distraction. The words were similar to Washington's speech stating the con- viction in God can be better than faith in government. God was the tool used to limit Governmental overreach in Ameri- ca, and they believed it can work in the new post Berlin Wall USSR. Washington said to forbid a national morality over an exclusion of religious principles. This was as true for America as it was for Russia, a once highly religious country.

Let's look at further Presidential policies...
One policy that took people by surprise is that under the Carter administration our government decided to boycott an Olympic competition that for hundreds of years mankind diligently participated.

We decided to follow along as a country with our President to try and keep America out of another war. We do not have Americans boycotting the Olympics in the past couple de- cades because of politics, as we did during the Carter years. In 1980, our leaders thought it would change the hearts of irrational men in the USSR's government by boycotting the Olympics. The entire world was upset about the USSR's aggression in Afghanistan. President Trump's policies helped to save the Olympics from our political adversary of North Korea, and these games continued as a globally participated event. Forgoing competing in an Olympic event did nothing but disappoint and disheartened the athletes who trained for the four years prior.

Our problems as a country cannot be fixed without our government officials acknowledging them.

President Carter gave away the Panama Canal for one dollar, while tens of thousands of Americans died building it. We have undoubtedly the biggest and most powerful military in the world's history yet, we backed out of the Vietnam War and evacuated from the Afghanistan War leaving a giant military installation that cost Americans billions of dollars, and it was useful to stop Chinese aggressive movements towards the West. What this has become are the contrasts in these rules of political thought, one has an uplifting positive outcome and the other is Democratic politics.

Lets look into a positive outcome presidency...
A look at President's policies and how they helped every America would be to glance at President Bush (43) administration. President Bush was hit early in his presidency with a lagging economy, brought on by the dot com bust and the 911 terrorist plot, and sought out new ways to get America to look forward to another four years of his presidency.

President Bush got the tax relief bill signed into law and *the US saw 52 months of uninterrupted job growth*, a new record. His ideas of letting Americans keep more of their own money through the tax relief package got companies to hire more people thus, those Americans could buy more products that drove the our consumption-related economy.

As families flourished, the taxes were dropped for them by giving families child tax credits. It also reduced the marriage tax penalty and parked the death tax at its lowest level ever. Finally, businesses were able to take a quadrupled tax relief for expenses of doing their business. This created an economy that grew an average of 7.5% over inflation.

A Generational trend of Disillusionment in
Americans is not an inescapable trend.

Chapter Two

the1960s started what unfurls into today.

Living in the early and middle 60s era felt like we as a nation were still living as it was the 1950s when America was ultimately the World's economic power after WWII. America's failures in Korea and Vietnam created a power vacuum that still exists in every aspect of our world's society. Many people are unsure about America's future as the Cold War still hangs on with renewed and continued aggression from mother Russia.

The 1960s evolved in America and across the world, a stand against the traditional bureaucratic powers by our youth grew. The generation of music and experimentation in drugs started to question the norms of the 1950s. Our 60s youth were fiercely against the war. This is how our 1960s experiment and dilemma frames the direction of the way we live today.

Our disillusionment of today was built from what we endured in the 1960s and again in the 1970s.
Disillusionment expansion of the 1960s -
here is an overview.

The 1960s, especially under President Lyndon B. Johnson, saw a major expansion of the federal bureaucracy due to the Great Society programs aimed at fighting poverty and promoting civil rights, healthcare, and education.

Federal employment grew to about 2.2 million, and new agencies like Medicare and the Office of Economic Opportunity were established to manage these programs. The bureaucracy became more involved in direct service provision to the public, with a focus on social welfare and regulatory roles.

Growth slowed after the 1960s, but new agencies like the Environmental Protection Agency (EPA) and Occupational Safety and Health Administration (OSHA) were created in the 1970s.

Criticism of bureaucratic inefficiency led to reforms, such as the Freedom of Information Act (1966) and Government in Sunshine Act (1976), aimed at increasing transparency and accountability.

The number of managerial layers in government increased dramatically, a phenomenon known as "thickening government." The average number of layers between the president and frontline workers rose from 17 in 1960 to 32 in 1992, with more political appointees and senior managers.

Privatization and Contracting (1980s–1990s)

The 1980s and 1990s saw a political push, especially from conservatives, to reduce the size and direct role of government, leading to increased privatization and outsourcing of government functions.

The Clinton administration in the 1990s, with Vice President Al Gore, aggressively pursued shrinking the federal workforce and embracing privatization, a trend supported across party lines at the time.

Fewer civil servants interacted directly with the public, as more services were delivered via contracts with private companies and mandates to state and local governments.

Summary: Key Changes (1960–1990)

*   Era/Aspect, 1960s Expansion
*   1970s–1980s: Reform & Critique
*   In the 1990s: Privatization & Downsizing
*   Size: Major growth (2.2M workers), growth slows, new agencies added. Workforce shrinks, more outsourcing.

- Focus: Social programs, regulation.
- Efficiency: transparency.
- Privatization: managerial oversight.
- Structure: direct service provision. More managerial layers.
- Fewer front-line workers, more contracts.
- Political Attitude, support for expansion.
- Rising skepticism, bipartisan support for downsizing.

Overall, U.S. bureaucracy from 1960 to 1990 shifted from rapid expansion and direct service provision to a focus on managerial oversight, transparency, and ultimately, privatization and outsourcing of many government functions.

That's a concise and insightful overview of the significant shifts in the U.S. bureaucracy between 1960 and 1990. You've clearly highlighted the key trends and contributing factors for each era. The summary table effectively consolidates the main changes across size, focus, structure, and political attitude.

It's interesting to see how the initial expansion driven by the Great Society programs gave way to a period of critique and reform, ultimately leading to a bipartisan push for privatization and downsizing by the 1990s. The "thickening government" phenomenon you mentioned is a crucial structural change that likely had significant impacts on efficiency and communication within the bureaucracy.

Do you have any specific questions about these changes or would you like to explore any particular aspect in more detail? For example, we could delve into the specific impacts of privatization, the long-term consequences of the increased managerial layers, or the evolution of public perception towards the bureaucracy during this period.

Disillusionment is not a difference of opinion, it becomes a difference of principles. That is how Thomas Jefferson put it to the American people, who saw his new and different political party taking over from the previous American administrations. After all the fighting and back room deals the administrations decided to disagree as friends and then found an outcome that helped Americans come together as a people. American Disillusionment can be seen as a theatrical play.

Over the past few decades, you have the first act of the 1960s, the middle is the 70s and the conclusion of the play are the 1990s which has laid groundwork for the new ideals of today's culture. So much has changed in this era, it can't be compared to others. Our governmental bureaucracy is not perfect in any circumstance, and most times our government gets it wrong. Exemplified by those famous words of

President Reagan as he expressed it best: the 11 most dangerous words in our language are: "Hello, I am from the government, we are here to help". Some words can not be exemplified as well as when Regan said them, which he pointed out the biggest problem we have is the one that is suppose to be our life-saver.

Politicians who mimic President Kennedy and Reagan's speeches have done well. In my era, President Kennedy led the way to acquire American hearts and minds as he pursued words of encouragement and sometimes challenge ("let's be the ones to send the first person to the Moon"). We should all take advantage of the strength of our government and, at the same time; be aware of how all-powerful it can be against us. Look at Hillary Clinton's plan to spy on a current president and then with the government's help try to blame that same person for these actions that were taken against him. After America found out about her, destroying all evidence and flaunting her actions for everyone to see, she lost favor with all but a few Americans. The only segment of society that supported her were the American media outlets that led the Federal government to protect this criminal instead of sending her and her involved staff to trial.

The strength of our government is to keep us safe, it is its essential purpose. The way the government is now making it possible for people to invade our country should be a chilling reflection for many Americans. As the government contradicts this, we see daily pictures of hundreds of thousands of criminals breaking the law of our country and the country's government does not do anything. The only reason for this is to gain a new political advantage by ensuring these criminals become Americans that can vote for the politicians that supported them invading our country.

It seems as though history plays out like this in all instances of American Disillusionment. Initially, you have the era where an event happens. The next era legitimizes this evolution of American society, the next is how it can be used to alter the way we presently live.

An example of this is the 1980s Mariel boat lift from Cuba to Miami. The prevalent thought was that these illegals would always vote towards the party that gave them the ability to live here as Americans. What happened a decade or so later, these historically conservative minded people started to vote with their conscience and the decade's long rampant Democratic rule in South Florida turned red.

Here are some key impacts:
Demographic Changes: The boat lift brought approximately 125,000 Cuban refugees to the U.S., primarily to Miami. This influx significantly altered the demographic landscape of South Florida, leading to a substantial increase in the Cuban-American population.
Cultural Influence: The arrival of Cuban refugees contributed to the rich cultural tapestry of Miami and the broader

U.S. Cuban community. It led to the establishment of Cuban restaurants, businesses, and cultural institutions, influencing music, art, and cuisine in the region.

Political Impact: The Mariel Boat Lift had political ramifications, as it intensified discussions about U.S. immigration policy and relations with Cuba. It also influenced the political landscape in Florida, where Cuban-Americans became a significant voting bloc.

Economic Effects: The sudden influx of refugees posed challenges for local economies, including strain on social services and housing. However, many Cuban immigrants eventually contributed to the economy by starting businesses and filling labor shortages.

Public Perception and Media Coverage: The boat lift was marked by media coverage that often portrayed the refugees in a negative light, particularly due to the inclusion of some individuals released from Cuban prisons. This affected public perception and led to debates about immigration and refugee policies.

Long-term Immigration Policy: The events surrounding the Mariel Boat Lift influenced U.S. immigration policy, leading to changes in how refugees and asylum seekers were processed and perceived in the years that followed.

Overall, the Mariel Boat Lift was a pivotal event that shaped the Cuban-American experience and had lasting effects on U.S. society and policy.

Disillusionment surfaces as the realization of previous victories or conclusions that changed American lives are now seen as disappointing in their conclusion because of the approach used. We are now seeing the results of a weak presidency's actions can be turned into positive results for Americans after the right direction is taken by the next president.

Take the Civil Rights movement. At the time, everyone was happy to be involved, but today, its emerging impact is seen as an erroneous entitlement circumstance for a segment of the electorate. Over the years, this has continuously separated us along party lines, thus setting an inclination to vote for our individual partisan half of our democracy. It is what becomes of us as a Nation in spite of these natural human tendencies to make America better again and again.

What are the signs of disillusionment? Progressing from the 1950s to the 1960s, what was a commonplace paradigm of this American era.

Disillusionment arises when life experiences strongly discredited positive assumptions or deeply held beliefs. Under these conditions, people feel lost, confused, and disconnected from their social previous held thoughts. This was on full display in the 1960s across every society component as the media outlets across America highlighted them every night on National television.

The Sixties movements led to Disillusionment:
In the later 1960s, disillusionment was seen in the youth of America. As they gain more and more power with their votes, America turns inside out, seemingly living in two separate realities. Lost forever is the pride of being an American of the 1950s. Living in the 60s was like waking from a deceptive illusion.

This is the time when strong American leadership was needed to unite us and strengthen the indispensable role our country plays for the health and safety of the world.

Major Changes in American Social Issues (1950–1970)

Civil Rights Movement:

The 1950s and 1960s saw a powerful push for racial equality, culminating in landmark events such as the Brown v. Board of Education decision (1954), the Montgomery Bus Boycott (1955), and the March on Washington (1963). The Civil Rights Act (1964) and Voting Rights Act (1965) legally ended segregation and protected voting rights for African Americans.

Women's Rights:

The women's movement gained momentum, with increased advocacy for workplace equality, reproductive rights, and legal reforms. The publication of "The Feminine Mystique" (1963) and the founding of the National Organization for Women (1966) were pivotal moments.

Purpose of the National Organization for Women (1966)

The National Organization for Women (NOW) was founded in 1966 to take action to bring women into full participation in the mainstream of American society, exercising all privileges and responsibilities in truly equal partnership with men. The founders believed it was time to move beyond discussion and confront, with concrete action, the conditions preventing women from enjoying equality of opportunity and freedom of choice as their right, both as Americans and as human beings.

NOW aimed to:

- Achieve true equality for all women in America.
- Ensure women could participate fully in political, economic, and social life.
- Address and eliminate sex discrimination, especially in employment and education.
- Advocate for enforcement of existing anti-discrimination laws, such as Title VII of the Civil Rights Act of 1964.
- The organization was inspired by the broader human

rights movements of the era and sought to be a driving force for gender equality through activism, lobbying, and public advocacy.

LGBTQ+ Rights:

The period saw the beginnings of the LGBTQ+ rights movement, including the 1969 Stonewall Rebellion, which marked a turning point for gay rights activism.

Disability Rights:

Social security amendments in the 1950s and 1960s expanded aid for people with disabilities. The late 1960s and early 1970s saw the rise of disability rights activism, with organizations and protests advocating for inclusion and accessibility.

Anti-War and Student Movements:

The Vietnam War sparked widespread protest, especially among youth and students. The Free Speech Movement and anti-war demonstrations became central to campus life and national debate.

Economic Shifts and Suburbanization:

Postwar prosperity led to suburban growth, but also to increased economic disparity, especially along racial lines. While average incomes rose, Black families continued to earn significantly less than White families.

Environmental and Consumer Movements:

The first Earth Day in 1970 and the founding of organizations like Greenpeace signaled growing concern for environmental issues and consumer protection.

Summary of Key Social Issues:
- Civil Rights: Brown v. Board, bus boycotts.
- Voting Rights: Ongoing activism.
- Women's Rights:

- NOW founded: feminist literature .
- ERA passes Congress:
- LGBTQ+ Rights:
- Disability Rights:
- Social Security amendments:
- Activist groups form:
- Anti-War/Student: Vietnam protests and Free Speech
- Environmental: Limited awareness.
- Growing concern: First Earth Day, Greenpeace.

These decades transformed American society, laying the groundwork for ongoing struggles for equality, justice, and expanded rights.

A crisis of disillusionment where Americans fall away from a coherence of previous 1950's norms and their meaning, revealing a system of intertwined essentials that had always been lived within an implicit part of one's assumption of life, and that now seems handicapped, and offbeat.

Early in the 1960s, **President Kennedy** *- with Ask Not what your country can do FOR YOU....Asked America's youth to be more involved and seize their place in America's culture.*

This began with President Kennedy telling us our democracy's needs to be better and he began cataloging impressive achievements. In the early 60s, the media was live broadcasting Kennedy's new conferences. Kennedy became our first routinely televised president. After many unflattering issues were published in daily news reports, President Kennedy's Camelot started to flounder. As the media continued daily listing his administrations failures, he still had a consequential congregation of Americans believing in his policies.

The notion of "national" service becomes complex and contentious in this climate. It has Disillusionment brings about change. Change is inevitable; it often arrives as a disruption and a challenge to the status quo. This years election demonstrates to America that we can dream big and identify solutions for the issues that matter to us.

The erosion of trust reflects a deeper malaise within our society. We saw similar patterns during President Carter's administration in the 1970s. Over the last few decades, it appears that America has been increasingly at odds with itself. The political arena has turned into a battleground where partisan rhetoric frequently portrays the greatest threats to the country as internal (e.g., the "Swamp") rather than external.

In this climate, the concept of "national" service becomes complex and contentious. This idea was prominently highlighted in American politics during the 1960s, with President Kennedy using it as a rallying point a term and form of thought that the 1960s brought to the forefront of American politics of President Kennedy's term. America will always have the next new national thought be one of change. It is easy to disrupt malaise with change in governmental politics.

60 years after his homicide, the lesser-known facts delivered to the American public about his death continue to stun Americans into skepticism.

The Race to the Moon starts a new Era.
Our country's obsession with beating the USSR to the moon bound most American households to one another via watching spectacular television images. After failures in the NASA program,

The Race to the Moon refers to the competition between the United States and the Soviet Union during the Cold War to achieve significant milestones in space exploration, culminating in the Apollo 11 mission, which successfully landed humans on the Moon in 1969.

Key Events in the Race to the Moon:

Sputnik (1957): The Soviet Union launched Sputnik 1, the first artificial satellite, marking the beginning of the space age and the space race.

Vostok 1 (1961): Yuri Gagarin became the first human to orbit the Earth, further intensifying the competition.

Project Mercury (1958-1963): The United States' first human spaceflight program, which included the first American in space, Alan Shepard, in 1961.

Gemini Program (1962-1966): This program focused on developing space travel techniques and included missions that tested spacewalks and orbital maneuvers.

Apollo Program (1961-1972): Initiated by President John F. Kennedy's famous 1961 speech, where he declared the goal of landing a man on the Moon and returning him safely to Earth.

Key missions included:

Apollo 1: A tragic cabin fire during a pre-launch test in 1967 that killed three astronauts.

Impact of the Race to the Moon:

Technological Advancements: The space race led to significant advancements in technology, engineering, and materials science.

Political and Cultural Influence: The achievements in space exploration had a profound impact on national pride, international relations, and the public's interest in science and technology.

Legacy: The race to the Moon set the stage for future space exploration, including the development of the Space Shuttle program, the International Space Station, and ongoing missions to Mars and beyond.

The Race to the Moon remains a defining moment in human history, symbolizing the spirit of exploration and the quest for knowledge.

Kennedy was known as the 1960's president who boasted of "failing big to make big accomplishments." This became the time of Cuba's Bay of Pigs disgrace and we learned about Operation Paperclip.

Following his election in November 1960, President John F. Kennedy learned of the CIA's previously planned invasion of Cuba. President Kennedy gave his consent to the clandestine invasion of Cuba after learning that the Swamp of Washington was not going to change its goals.

We've faced worse: war, dismal economic times and upheaval, with our new national social transformation. In those moments, great leaders like Presidents Lincoln, Truman and Eisenhower guided Americans forward with common sense and pragmatism. It turns out that our best leaders do all they can to strengthen the bonds that unite us.

This soon to be disaster was launched from Guatemala, this government planned attack went wrong almost from the start. The US Brigade of 2,500 CIA-led combatants landed at the Bay of Pigs on April 17, 1961, and were defeated within 2 days by Cuban armed forces under the direct command of Castro. America for the first time watched on daily TV programs the newest national disillusionment.

The failed invasion strengthened the position of Castro's administration, which proceeded to openly proclaim its intention to adopt socialism and pursue closer ties with the Soviet Union, which brought about the Missile Crisis the next year for President Kennedy to bear.

In July 1962 Soviet premier Nikita Khrushchev reached a secret agreement with Cuban premier Fidel Castro to place Soviet nuclear missiles in Cuba to deter any future invasion attempt. Kennedy summoned his closest advisers to consider options and direct a course of action for the United States that would resolve the crisis. The conspicuous tone of the President's remarks directed at the USSR was stern, and the message was unmistakable, which advocated the Monroe Doctrine: "It shall be the policy of this nation to regard any nuclear missile launched from Cuba against any nation in the Western Hemisphere as an attack by the Soviet Union on the United States, requiring a full retaliatory response upon the Soviet Union."

Cuba again makes a difference in American politics.
The presence of Soviet nuclear missiles in Cuba was a central issue during the Cold War, particularly during the Cuban Missile Crisis in October 1962. This event marked a significant confrontation between the United States and the Soviet Union and is often considered one of the closest moments the world came to nuclear war.

Background:
Cuban Revolution: After Fidel Castro's revolution in 1959, Cuba became a communist state and aligned itself with the Soviet Union. This alignment was concerning for the United States, which viewed the spread of communism in the Western Hemisphere as a direct threat.
Soviet Support: In response to U.S. actions, including the failed Bay of Pigs invasion in 1961, the Soviet Union, led by Premier Nikita Khrushchev, decided to place nuclear missiles in Cuba. This was intended to deter further U.S. aggression and to level the strategic playing field, as the U.S. had nuclear missiles positioned in Turkey and Italy, within striking distance of the Soviet Union.

The Crisis:
Discovery: In October 1962, U.S. reconnaissance flights over Cuba revealed the presence of Soviet missile sites under construction. These missiles had the capability to strike major U.S. cities within minutes.

U.S. Response: President John F. Kennedy and his administration faced a critical decision. After consulting with his advisors, he opted for a naval blockade (termed a "quarantine")
of Cuba to prevent further shipments of military equipment
from the Soviet Union.

Tensions Escalate: The situation escalated as both super-
powers prepared for potential military confrontation. The
world watched anxiously as diplomatic negotiations took
place.

Resolution: Ultimately, a deal was reached. The Soviet Union
agreed to dismantle the missile sites in Cuba in exchange for
a U.S. promise not to invade Cuba and the secret removal of
U.S. missiles from Turkey. This resolution helped to de-esca-
late the immediate crisis.

Aftermath:

The Cuban Missile Crisis had lasting effects on U.S.-Soviet
relations and global politics. It led to:

Increased Communication: The establishment of a direct
communication line (the "hotline") between Washington and
Moscow to prevent future crises.

Nuclear Arms Control: A greater emphasis on arms control agreements, leading to treaties such as the Nuclear
Non-Proliferation Treaty (NPT) in 1968.

Shift in Cold War Dynamics: The crisis highlighted the dan-
gers of nuclear weapons and the need for careful diplomacy,
influencing U.S. and Soviet foreign policy in the years that
followed.

The Cuban Missile Crisis remains a pivotal moment in Cold
War history, illustrating the complexities of nuclear deterrence and international relations.

Then, in 1969, the Moon race was completed. Americans
were the first to land on the moon, but President Kennedy
never saw this accomplishment. Operation Paperclip was

discovered to be a US government secret in getting this accomplishment complete. It originated from the previous US president's strategies and was hidden from the American public. We then found out that our Moon Race success was based on America using hidden German Nazi scientists to formulate the space rocket program, as this other shoe dropped, America was disillusioned with their government under Kennedy's scrutiny once again.

Operation Paperclip and WTF:
Operation Paperclip brought WWII German scientists to America; because they were years ahead of their American and Soviet counterparts in fields like rocketry, aeronautics, and synthetic fuels. In the concluding months of the liberation of Europe, the Allies had only a few months to transfer a horde of scientists stationed in Eastern Germany to the US before those areas fell under Soviet control.

Operation Paperclip energized the American scientific establishment in its competition against its incipient Soviet rival at the dawn of the last Cold War. Recruits like Wernher von Braun – known as the Father of Space Travel – led a team filled with other German scientists to design the Saturn V rocket that brought the first humans to the moon. Without these scientists' advanced knowledge of rocketry and ballistic missiles, the United States might have lost the Space Race. Along these same lines, these heralded Scientists had been brazenly displayed in the German homeland.

Here in America, being hidden from the publics eye they felt weakened and not appreciated for their talents, and felt as though America owed them.

While Operation Paperclip contributed significantly to American scientific advancements, it was also controversial due to the ethical implications of employing individuals who had been involved in war crimes and human rights abuses during the Nazi regime. The program has been the subject of extensive historical research and debate regarding its moral and political ramifications.

This brought them out to seek power in governing if they could not assume the hero's welcome. Operation Paperclip operators trained their staff in the reality that they were still the superior faction in the government. Those leaders breed the next generation, and they started attaining positions of power in the government. After acquiring their post, they birthed an entire new segment in the political arena that has never gone away, it has just grown more powerful.

President Trump's "Swamp" might be the end result of this immigration and naturalization of the political class in America.

During times of disillusionment, Americans were saying the entire achievement (the Moon landing) was staged. The American public still had feelings of distrust, even at our great time of national achievement. As the Paperclip invasion into the political class expanded, it grabbed coveted positions throughout all parts of our government. These can be seen as positions in creating and growing bureaucracies, mostly creating a position where they can regulate over other bureaus that regulate entire sects of society.

Operation Paperclip also brought a dark and secret society of scientists to be based in the infamous Area 51. They were creating more than secret lives, they developed and delivered mass-produced technology engines to the world.

Operation Paperclip refers to several contexts, particularly in the fields of aerospace, automotive, or industrial machinery.

Aerospace: In the context of aerospace, this could refer to the development and mass production of jet engines or rocket engines. Companies like General Electric, Pratt & Whitney, and Rolls-Royce have been involved in creating advanced jet engines for commercial and military aircraft. Similarly, NASA and private companies like SpaceX have developed rocket engines for space exploration.

Automotive: In the automotive industry, this could refer to the mass production of internal combustion engines or electric powertrains. Major automotive manufacturers like Ford, Toyota, and Tesla have developed engines and powertrains that are produced at scale to meet consumer demand.

Industrial Machinery: In manufacturing, "technology engines" could refer to the development of machinery and equipment that drive production processes. This includes everything from assembly line robots to CNC machines that are mass-produced for various industries.

Software and Technology: In a more abstract sense, "technology engines" could also refer to software platforms or frameworks that drive technological innovation, such as cloud computing services or machine learning algorithms that are widely adopted and implemented across various sectors.

Chapter Three:
The Enduring Debacle.

LBJ .... And the Great Social Giveaways.

*Our Government giving away free stuff is the start of the
entitlement policies that are popular even today.
The new thinking....this rule of thought...subverts
personal responsibilities.
Giveaways create an entitlement that grew into an
awkward journey for the past 5 decades.*

A major initiative in the Lyndon Johnson presidency was the
Vietnam War. It was started to change communism's grasp
on Asia. By 1968, the United States had 548,000 troops in
Vietnam and had already lost 30,000 Americans there. Johnson's approval ratings had dropped from 70 percent in mid-
1965 to below 40 percent by 1967, and with it, his control of
Congress which made way to elect President Nixon, where
the war ended within his Presidency.

Lyndon B. Johnson and His Bureaucracy Expansion of
Federal Bureaucracy:
Lyndon B. Johnson's presidency (1963–1969) marked a major expansion of the federal bureaucracy, especially through
his ambitious "Great Society" agenda. Johnson oversaw the
most significant increase in federal employees, reaching 2.2
million, and a federal budget that soared to $332 billion by
the end of the 1960s.

He created new federal departments, such as the Department of Housing and Urban Development, and appointed the
first African American cabinet member, Robert Weaver, to
lead it.
Key Domestic Programs and Bureaucratic Growth
Johnson's "Great Society" programs aimed to eliminate pov-

erty and racial injustice, leading to the creation and expansion of federal agencies to manage new initiatives in education, healthcare, urban renewal, and civil rights.

Major programs included Medicare and Medicaid, which required new bureaucratic structures for implementation and oversight. The passage of the Civil Rights Act (1964), Voting Rights Act (1965), and Executive Order 11246 (affirmative action) demanded increased federal enforcement and regulatory capacity, expanding the reach and complexity of the bureaucracy.

Role in Civil Rights and Equal Opportunity

Johnson's administration used the federal bureaucracy to enforce civil rights legislation and affirmative action, mandating federal contractors to take proactive steps against discrimination and imposing penalties for non-compliance. The interplay between the presidency, Congress, and the federal bureaucracy was crucial in implementing and sustaining these sweeping changes.

Legacy

Johnson's legacy is closely tied to the growth and power of the federal bureaucracy, both praised for advancing social welfare and criticized for expanding government reach and complexity.

While his domestic achievements are significant, his presidency is also remembered for the controversial expansion of federal power and the Vietnam War.

The Vietnam War played a major role in the 1970s malaise by deeply undermining Americans' trust in their government and sense of national purpose. The war's prolonged, costly, and ultimately unsuccessful outcome shattered the image of the U.S. as an unbeatable superpower, leading to widespread doubt about America's global role and military effectiveness.

At home, the war fueled intense social divisions, mass protests, and a powerful anti-war movement, exposing and deepening rifts within American society. Revelations of government deception, such as the Pentagon Papers, and the trauma of returning veterans further eroded public confidence. The war's legacy left Americans questioning their leaders, their country's moral standing, and their ability to shape world events, all of which contributed to the era's pervasive sense of malaise.

President Johnson & the Vietnam War

The U.S. was already involved in Vietnam before Johnson Eisenhower and especially Kennedy had sent military advisors to help South Vietnam fight against the communist North (led by Ho Chi Minh).

It was part of the Cold War — the U.S. feared the "domino theory": that if one country fell to communism, others in Southeast Asia would follow.

Gulf of Tonkin Incident (August 1964):
U.S. Navy ships were allegedly attacked by North Vietnamese boats in the Gulf of Tonkin.
• Johnson used this incident to rally Congress.

Gulf of Tonkin Resolution:
Passed almost unanimously by Congress.
• Gave LBJ broad military powers in Vietnam without an official declaration of war.

This is what effectively "sent America to War" — and, it escalated fast.

Escalation of the War:
By 1965, Johnson sent ground troops — starting with 3,500 Marines.

Eventually, over 500,000 U.S. troops were in Vietnam.

- Bombing campaigns like Operation Rolling Thunder devastated the North.
- The war dragged on for years with heavy casualties, unclear objectives, and growing public opposition.

Public Backlash & Legacy:

Johnson's popularity plummeted as the war dragged on. The anti-war movement exploded protests, draft dodging, and national division.

- He chose not to run for re-election in 1968, partly because of how unpopular the war had become.
- Vietnam damaged his legacy, even though he passed landmark civil rights and social welfare laws at home (e.g., Civil Rights Act, Medicare).

Lyndon B. Johnson escalated the Vietnam War after the Gulf of Tonkin incident, using a congressional resolution to massively increase U.S. military involvement even though Congress never officially declared war. It became one of the most controversial wars in American history.

'Nam did what to 'merica?

The Vietnam War contributed to the decline in trust in government primarily through the emergence of a "credibility gap"—the growing perception that government officials were not telling the truth about the war's progress and intentions. Presidents and military leaders repeatedly assured the public of imminent victory and downplayed setbacks, but media coverage and events like the Tet Offensive revealed a much grimmer reality, exposing contradictions between official statements and actual conditions.

This gap widened further with the release of the Pentagon Papers in 1971, which documented years of government deception about the war's scope and prospects. The public learned that leaders had misled both Congress and citizens,

fueling cynicism and a lasting distrust of government authority. As a result, the Vietnam War is widely seen as a turning
point that "killed trust" in American institutions and made the
public more skeptical of official narratives.

Dems during the war...
The Vietnam War split the Democratic Party by creating
a deep divide between its pro-war "hawks" and anti-war
"doves." Initially, most Democrats supported an assertive foreign policy, but as the war dragged on and casualties mounted, a powerful anti-war movement emerged within the party.

Key ways the split manifested:
1968 Presidential Election: President Lyndon Johnson's
escalation of the war alienated many Democrats, leading
anti-war Senator Eugene McCarthy to challenge him in the
primaries. Johnson's withdrawal from the race, the assassination of Robert F. Kennedy, and the chaotic, protest-filled
Democratic National Convention in Chicago exposed the
party's internal rifts.
Party Realignment: Many blue-collar and working-class
Democrats, frustrated by the party's growing anti-war stance,
began to drift away, some becoming independents or Republicans. The party's traditional coalition of Southerners, labor,
and urban ethnic voters fractured, weakening its electoral
strength.
Long-term Impact: The split over Vietnam led to the nomi-
nation of anti-war candidate George McGovern in1972, but
many in the party's traditional base did not support him,
resulting in a landslide loss to Richard Nixon. The divide between the party's grassroots doves and establishment hawks
persisted for decades, shaping Democratic foreign policy
debates.
In summary, the Vietnam War was the catalyst that exposed
and deepened ideological, generational, and regional divisions within the Democratic Party, fundamentally altering its
coalition and political trajectory.

Dems split...

The main arguments of the anti-war and pro-war factions within the Democratic Party during the Vietnam War era were as follows:

Anti-War Faction ("Doves")

Moral and Human Cost: Argued the war was unjust, immoral, and resulted in unnecessary loss of life for both Americans and Vietnamese.

Ineffectiveness: Believed the war was un-winnable and that continued involvement would only prolong suffering without achieving meaningful results.

Domestic Priorities: Asserted that resources spent on the war should be redirected to address pressing social issues at home, such as poverty and civil rights.

Distrust of Government: Pointed to government deception (e.g., the Pentagon Papers) and the "credibility gap" as reasons to end U.S. involvement.

International Reputation: Warned that the war damaged America's standing in the world and fueled anti-American sentiment.

Pro-War Faction ("Hawks")

Containment of Communism: Supported the war as necessary to prevent the spread of communism in Southeast Asia, adhering to the "domino theory."

U.S. Credibility: Argued that withdrawal would undermine U.S. credibility with allies and embolden adversaries.

Support for Allies: Believed the U.S. had a responsibility to support South Vietnam against communist aggression.

National Unity and Patriotism: Framed opposition to the war as unpatriotic and potentially harmful to troop morale and national unity.

Gradual Reform: Some hawks believed reforms in South Vietnam could be achieved through continued U.S. support and military presence.

These opposing arguments led to deep divisions within the Democratic Party, shaping its internal debates and electoral fortunes throughout the late 1960s and 1970s.

Divided Dems...

The Democratic Party's divisions over the Vietnam War had several long-term impacts on its political strategy:

Fragmented Coalition: The split between anti-war "doves" and pro-war "hawks" fractured the party's traditional coalition, especially alienating working-class and rural voters who felt disconnected from the party's increasingly liberal, urban, and anti-war base. This realignment contributed to the party's growing concentration in urban areas and among more educated, diverse, and liberal constituencies.

Ideological Polarization: The internal conflict accelerated the party's shift to the left, as anti-war and progressive voices gained influence. Over time, this led to greater ideological polarization between Democrats and Republicans, with less overlap and more partisan animosity.

Strategic Dilemmas: The party has since struggled to balance the demands of its diverse and sometimes competing factions—progressives, moderates, minorities, and working-class voters—making it harder to craft a unified message and broad-based electoral strategy. Debates continue over whether to pursue popular, centrist policies or a more robust progressive agenda.

Urban-Rural Divide: The Vietnam-era split contributed to a long-term urban-rural divide, with Democrats becoming more associated with urban, diverse, and progressive interests, while losing ground in rural and working-class communities.

The Vietnam War divisions set the stage for decades of internal debate, demographic change, and strategic challenges that continue to shape the Democratic Party's identity and electoral approach today.

Compare early democrats to now

The Democratic Party has undergone significant changes since its early days in the early 19th century. Below are several key points of comparison between early Democrats and the modern Democratic Party:

Origins and Ideology:

Early Democrats: The Democratic Party was founded in the 1820s, evolving from the Democratic-Republican Party of Thomas Jefferson. Early Democrats were typically agrarian, favoring states' rights, individual liberties, and a limited federal government. Major figures, such as Andrew Jackson, championed populist ideals and were often seen as representatives of the "common man."

Modern Democrats: Today's Democratic Party has shifted towards a platform that advocates for a more active role of the federal government in economic and social issues. Modern Democrats typically embrace social justice, environmental protection, and a mixed economy, balancing private enterprise with government regulation.

Key Issues:

Early Democrats: Early party priorities often included westward expansion, states' rights, and opposition to the national bank. They were also largely associated with the pro-slavery stance in the pre-Civil War era and maintained strong support in the Southern states.

Modern Democrats: The contemporary platform emphasizes civil rights, social equality, healthcare access, climate change action, and economic equity. The party has largely distanced itself from its historical support for slavery and segregation.

Demographics:

Early Democrats: The base was predominantly rural, with strong support in the South and among white males, particularly landowners and farmers.

Modern Democrats: The current Democratic Party has a

more diverse coalition, including significant support from urban populations, minority groups, women, and younger voters. The party actively seeks to address issues of racial and gender equality.

Party Organization:

Early Democrats: The structure was less formal, with local party organizations and a more decentralized approach. Politics were often personal and community-based.

Modern Democrats: The party has a more structured organization with formal leadership at local, state, and national levels. Campaigns rely heavily on data, technology, and media outreach to engage voters.

Electoral Trends:

Early Democrats: The party faced significant challenges, including fragmentation over issues like slavery, leading to the Civil War and a split that produced the Confederacy.

Modern Democrats: After the Civil Rights Movement, which saw a major realignment of party support, Democrats became more progressive on social issues. They now often face challenges such as polarization, partisanship, and competition from other parties, like the Republican Party.

....And:

The Democratic Party has transformed from its early roots as a champion of agrarian interests and states' rights to a modern party that emphasizes social justice, equality, and federal responsibility in addressing contemporary issues. This evolution reflects broader shifts in American society and values over the past two centuries.

The main difference between Democrats and Republicans
is their political philosophies, policies, and approaches to government.

Here is a basic breakdown of the two major political parties in the United States:

Democrats: (Left-leaning / Liberal / Progressive)

Government Role: Believe that the federal government should take a more active role in addressing social issues.

Taxes: In general, I support raising taxes on the wealthy in order to fund social programs.

Healthcare: Support government involvement in healthcare (e.g., the Affordable Care Act and Medicare expansion).

Social Issues: Support abortion rights, LGBTQ+ rights, and stricter gun control.

Climate Change: Prioritize action on climate change and environmental regulation.

Economic Policy: I support raising the minimum wage, strengthening labor protections, and increasing regulation of big business.

Republicans (Right-leaning / Conservative)

Government Role: Support a smaller federal government with more power delegated to states and individuals.

Taxes: Generally support lower taxes, especially for businesses and high earners.

Healthcare: Prefer private-sector solutions over government involvement.

Social Issues: More conservative—frequently opposes abortion rights and supports gun rights.

Climate Change: Some members support action, but the party as a whole is less aggressive about environmental regulation.

Economic Policy: Emphasize free market policies, deregulation, and reducing government spending.

<u>In Practice:</u>

Not everyone in each party agrees with the party line, and there is a broad spectrum within each—for example, progressives vs. moderates in the Democratic Party and traditional conservatives vs. populists in the Republican Party.

Want a real-life example to see how their approaches differ on a topic like healthcare, immigration, or education?

What is the difference in Democrats from 1970s to 2025:
Political parties change dramatically over time, and the Democratic Party in the 1970s looked very different from the one in 2025. Here is a breakdown of some of the main changes:

Democrats in the 1970s:
Socially: The party was in transition. It had supported civil rights in the 1960s, but it still had a mix of liberal Northerners and more conservative Southern Democrats (a group known as "Dixiecrats").
Economically, they are strongly pro-labor and pro-union, with a preference for New Deal-style government initiatives. The party supported regulation of big business and progressive taxation.
Race and Civil Rights: Officially supportive of civil rights, but Southern Democrats opposed racial integration and equality efforts, causing internal conflict. as
Foreign Policy: The party was divided over the Vietnam War. By the mid-1970s, many Democrats had grown increasingly skeptical of foreign military intervention.
Religious Influence: Religion, particularly Christianity, continued to play a significant role in Democratic identity, especially in the South.

Democrats in 2025:
Socially: Much more united around progressive social values—strongly pro-LGBTQ+ rights, pro-choice, and support for racial and gender equality.
Economically, the party continues to support labor and working-class issues, but there is a stronger emphasis on climate change, universal healthcare, student debt relief, and tech regulation.
Demographics: The party's base has shifted, with a stronger showing in urban areas among young people, minorities,

and college-educated voters. Southern conservatives who were once Democrats have mostly switched to the Republican party.

Foreign policy is generally cautious about military intervention, favoring diplomacy, human rights, and global cooperation.

Less emphasis on religion, with a focus on secular and inclusive values. A strong emphasis on diversity, equity, and inclusion.

Biggest Changes

Issue: Democrats from 1970s to 2025.

Race, still coping with the civil rights shift. Strongly pro-racial equity.

LGBTQ+Rarely discussed, but significant platform issue.

Economic Policy New Deal legacy, unions, Climate + tech economy focus.

Party Base, Working class, South, Urban, diverse, college-educated.

Culture, More moderate on social issues. More progressive overall.

What was the original political thesis of democrates?

Great question! The Democratic Party's original political thesis dates back to the early 1800s, and it has evolved significantly over time. However, if we return to the founding ideas, the main thesis was something like this:

"Power to the people, not the elite."

Here's how that looked when the Democratic Party really began to take shape:

Early Democratic Party (1820s–1840s)

Founded by supporters of Andrew Jackson, who became president in 1829.

Core Belief: Protect the "common man" (especially farmers

and laborers) from wealthy elites and centralized government power.

Government Role: Opposed a strong federal government (particularly a national bank), and advocated for state sovereignty.

Economics: Anti-monopoly, anti-bank, and pro-small business/agriculture.

Voters: Mostly white, rural, Southern, and Western men, particularly from the working classes.

Core Early Ideas: *Theme Belief*

Democracy, Expand voting rights (for white men) and lessen elitist control.

The anti-elite movement opposes banks, big government, and the ruling elite.

States' Rights: The federal government's role should be limited; most issues should be decided by the states.

Agrarian Focus: The ideal American was an independent farmer or laborer.

Early Democrats defended slavery and opposed civil rights for Black Americans. The party was deeply divided throughout history, and by the twentieth century, its thesis had shifted dramatically, particularly during and after the New Deal (1930s) and Civil Rights Movement (1960s).

<u>Now we see:</u>

The original thesis was to protect the little guy from elite power, but it was limited to white men and based on a very different social structure than today.

By 2025, the party's thesis has evolved into something more like: "Equality, inclusion, and government intervention to safeguard the vulnerable."

<u>The Media...</u>

The media played a pivotal role in shaping public opinion about the Vietnam War by bringing uncensored, graphic coverage directly into American homes, especially through television. This was the first war where people could regularly see real-time images of combat, casualties, and the hardships faced by soldiers and civilians, making the conflict immediate and personal for millions.

As the war progressed, media coverage shifted from initially supporting official government narratives to highlighting the growing gap between official statements and the realities on the ground. Iconic moments—such as the televised coverage of the Tet Offensive and the reporting of atrocities like the My Lai Massacre—contradicted government claims of imminent victory and exposed the brutality of the conflict, fueling public skepticism and anti-war sentiment.

Trusted journalists, notably Walter Cronkite, publicly questioned the likelihood of U.S. success, which further swayed public opinion and increased pressure on political leaders to change course. The media's investigative reporting and willingness to challenge official accounts contributed to a broader decline in trust in government and played a significant role in mobilizing the anti-war movement and shaping the national debate over U.S. involvement in Vietnam.

Johnson's prolific government spending programs and the start of the Vietnam War were never paid for by his raising of taxes, which led to our debt burden, and its inflationary tendencies which aided in the fatal culmination of President Carter's administration.

President Carter, thought of as America's worst president until Biden, told Americans we should accept this new downward trajectory of America. Our disillusionment in American life was on worldwide display during his televised State of the Union address. Disillusionment should have been his motto for his entire presidency. The Malaise was finally broken after President Carter left office and the American hostages were released from Iran under the presidency of Ronald Reagan. America entered a new beginning of social capacity, doubled with an economic boom because of the strength in President Reagan's governing policies.

Hostage release starts the re-tailoring of America.

Starting on shaky ground was the only way to start any initiative to free the hostages. The people of Iran were taken over by a prevailing, strong religious sect. After the leader of Iran had to escape to the US for medical attention, the country fell rapidly into a tyrannical seizure. It wasn't long before the hostages capture and retention was a daily feature in the American media.

Our paralyzed country and incapable military was on display for the world to see for 444 straight days.

The rapidly occurring events that unfolded caught the Carter presidency flat-footed. Not able to grasp the severity of the happenings in a distant land, President Carter misled America every day where nationally as a people we fell into a deeper despair. 444 days later, the oil-rich, Middle Eastern country's funds were released. Carter left Washington, DC, shaken and disgraced, but America was getting back on track with a new era of tactful presidential power and wisdom.

Soon after ... 1970's - Changing gender roles:

As American purchasing power and bravado increases, everyday Americans learn they need dual incomes to support the 1970s household. It was becoming more common to be a part of a broken divorced family as well. In 1960, 70 percent of American family homes had a parent that stayed home. Now, 70 percent of modern American families have both parents weekly working. This change in daily family life changed all of American society. In these times, American television commonly broadcasts shows that heralded single moms and their teenage motherhood to show this was normal American life.

Many women were driven into the marketplace in the 1970s. Still being discouraged by the considerable wage gap percentages between the genders, most American (65%) households have women as the breadwinner. Their wages were increasingly more important in every family to keep the American dream a reality. At the time of Kennedy's presidency, women were averaging 58 cents to the dollar earned by men.

In the 1960s, the wage gap between men and women in the United States was significant, reflecting broader societal norms and discrimination in the workplace. While exact percentages can vary based on the source and specific year, here are some general figures that illustrate the wage gap during that decade:

Early 1960s: In 1960, women earned approximately 60% of what men earned. This figure varied by occupation and region, but it provides a general sense of the disparity. Mid-1960s: By 1965, the wage gap had not changed significantly, with women earning about 62% of men's earnings. The Equal Pay Act of 1963 aimed to address wage discrimination, but its impact was gradual.

Late 1960s: By 1969, women were earning around 68% of what men earned. This increase was partly due to the growing number of women entering the workforce and the gradual changes in societal attitudes toward women's roles.
Factors Contributing to the Wage Gap.
Occupational Segregation: Women were often concentrated in lower-paying jobs and industries, such as teaching, nursing, and clerical work, while men dominated higher-paying fields like engineering and management.
Discrimination: Gender discrimination in hiring, promotions, and pay was widespread, limiting women's opportunities for

advancement and fair compensation.

Part-Time Work: Many women worked part-time or in temporary positions, which typically paid less than full-time jobs.

Societal Norms: Traditional gender roles influenced career choices and expectations, often discouraging women from pursuing higher-paying professions.

Progress Over Time:

The wage gap has narrowed since the 1960s, but disparities still exist today. Efforts to promote equal pay and address discrimination continue, with various laws and initiatives aimed at closing the gap further. The conversation around gender pay equity remains an important issue in contemporary discussions about workplace equality.

Women distrusted the workplace so much that this issue hasn't seen equity for women, even in today's marketplace.

Women's Lib was chaperoned by these changes:

The modern workplace gave women the ability to challenge salary discrepancies, as it crushed out-of-date norms with the constant freeing of women's issues in the present American sisterhood. At this time it was a standard practice of the family unit to be led by the father of the house. Women's lib said why and a matter of fact, we never did agree to that. It was this need not to conform that pushed women's lib to everyday media. Their old political references were no longer seen in mass media. Now it was cool to be the norm breaker.

Women as a group mostly distrusted the norms of the 1950s for good reason. It was this era where declining norms replaced desires in equating how Americans stridently could be better. As Americans broke from the bounds of previous social blueprints, new ways and different approaches to thinking about: what should be our way of life were the norm. There was not a problem that could not be talked about more widely than equality for women in every aspect of society. The 70s brought a feel that America's social Malaise could be solved if women lib continued to grow and break all barriers.

The 1970s saw growth in women's abilities to defend their rights as a group. Laws and events that took place in the 1970s and afterward helped. After President Johnson used the affirmative action policy (1967) to help Black Americans, he extended those rights to all women. Then 1968 the EEOC opened the way for all women to pursue high paying jobs that previously only men could attain. Who can forget the Battle of the Sexes in 1973. Billie Jean King beat Bobby Riggs to help affirm the Title 9 ruling that women's sports are treated equally across educational forums. Then later, after Sally Ride became the first woman astronaut, there was little doubt that women were capable and willing to do anything to be equals. Walter Mondale ran for the Presidency with Geraldine Ferraro as his vice president candidate. President Bill Clinton nominated our country's first woman attorney General. President Clinton also signed the Violence Against Women Act into law. Nancy Pelosi became our first female Speaker of the House in 2007. And in 2016, Hillary Clinton ran for President of the United States. 2021 saw Kamala Harris sworn in as this country's first vice President. 2024 saw this same woman run for President of the United States.

Stay at home Dads.
With the advent of the new 1980s era, it seemed normal for families to have a stay-at-home dad.

The 1980s began the ideal that fathers could stay at home to be with their families. The permanence of American families' achievement was rather small, but with the advent of the 2021 COVID-19 virus, the percentage of men staying at home went up to 30 percent in America.

This trend is repeating now, It is up over 8% over 1989. Dual income families have become the norm in the 2020s, and there is great news that flows with this. Women's salaries have increased enough to be able to have the family fathers stay at home and not work outside the home. It makes sense these days with the cost of child daycare escalating so much over the past decade. Everything from having a criminal record (and not able to get a job because of it) to drug additions have been cited for this to cause a rise in men staying at home. The past decade's financial crisis has pushed many 40-year-old men from the ranks of the employed. They have found getting back into their chosen occupation has been taken by younger, more agile (not bound with family issues) men straight out of college willing to accept less than a man that has midlife financial factors.

The Malaise of the 1980s was having too much of a good thing, and that brought in families to the "burbs". These moves were driven by the needs of the family. Dads stayed at home to care for his aging parents or, to be a better hands-on parent. It gave rise to separatism and depression in some dads that didn't have contact with the outside work world. Others did not buy into the stamp of: "something must be wrong with him". The redefining of the word baby sitting to caregiver gave many men the pride needed to get by the stigmatize of peers and neighbors.

Men that didn't have to work and stayed home to raise the kids, became a for friendly competition between other fathers in a community. A rivalry emerged, who can do everything for the family and have the best yard, car and a swimming pool to boot. The American economy realized that a woman's place could be in the 1980s workplace. Dad got to see what it was like doing five jobs every day for no pay, and they grew to love it.

As the previous macho eras of the 1950s passed, women became more sure of themselves and began raising their standings in the avocation of community. An ardent electorate as women became more confident in their power when organized and began to change America. As this 80s morale improved and grew, there were many national queries into electing a woman president or vice president. We have seen now many localities send female representatives into a once male-dominated realism.

Pulling in the Forgotten Black American:
Afro-Americans have merged into the heights of prominence never portrayed before in this country.
In the early 70s, Black Americans were used as pawns in our government's political game of Civil Rights.

The Civil Rights Movement in the United States was a complex and multifaceted struggle for racial equality and justice, primarily during the 1950s and 1960s. While many Black Americans were at the forefront of this movement, advocating for their rights and fighting against systemic racism, there were also instances where political leaders and institutions used the movement for their own agendas.

Some argue that certain politicians and organizations co-opted the Civil Rights Movement to gain political capital, distract from other issues, or to present a more favorable image of the United States during the Cold War. This included efforts to portray the U.S. as a champion of democracy and human rights, especially in contrast to the Soviet Union.

Additionally, the movement faced significant opposition, and many activists were subjected to violence, discrimination, and repression. The struggle for civil rights was not just a political game; it was a deeply personal and often dangerous fight for dignity, equality, and justice. The struggle for civil rights was a multifaceted movement that transcended mere political maneuvering. It was a deeply human endeavor aimed at achieving justice, equality, and dignity for all individuals, regardless of their race or background.

It's important to recognize the agency of Black Americans in this movement, as they were not merely pawns but active participants who shaped the course of history through their courage and resilience. The legacy of the Civil Rights Movement continues to influence contemporary discussions about race, justice, and equality in the United States.

When busing became a scourge upon America, this single issue tore American families apart. American children were forced to believe that sending them out of their familiar hometowns to neighborhoods that felt foreign was the new and the only way America perchance equalize the American experience between the races. This might have been avoided, but the brain-trust politicians impelled this theory to make a better American society. It could not and did not.

1973 and 1974, our current President, Joe Biden, began voting for many of the Senate's anti-busing bills, claiming that he favored school desegregation but objected to "forced busing". This was just another time when our government leaders were forced to fix a self-inflicted snafued political issue that ultimately led to another American Malaise. This and the need for self-righteous leadership to help others less fortunate than many Americans brought on the next Malaise to the same cultural segment.

It always felt that the 1960s Civil Rights movement fell short on the most important issues....

Equity in household wealth and workplace respect was never fully given to Black Americans in this movement. Most black American fell into a never ending cycle of poverty. The bureaucrats only knew how to make more bureaucracies. So providing housing to the less fortunate made a self-righteous proclamation to each of the virtues in the bureaucracies. This cycle boasts you can rely upon your fellow Americans to help you up. The way society's morals and ethics changed was the biggest Malaise in black America. Society tries to help with the goals, but every time the government helps, it gives the green light to people to be less self-reliant. This natural progression towards needing the government to pay the way of this new society of reliance has given the people who thought up these programs the power of their future vote. Remember Operation Paperclip, the scientist wanted to create a powerful throne in which to lead. This program makes it possible to encourage voting for those who support these abhorrent and controlling policies.

Many businesses have tried to bolster justness in their company's social aspects and how they treat the hiring practices of Black Americans. Most have fallen short during the 1970s and 80s. Many businesses have seen they can not compete with a government that ensures and helps bolster failure as it leads to expansion in the desire for unemployment. While unemployable, the government makes sure an American (and now illegals living in America) can get into several programs to feed, school, house and cloth you. All you have to do is not try and succeed into the American dream. Businesses have found they have to offer programs the government can not to get needed workers. Many now offer child care and bonuses for days of not missing their scheduled workdays.

Always and to a lesser measure, the American experience was not the same across the races. Black Americans smartly became more politically motivated to ensure their social and human rights were even-handed. As the staffing at local bureaucracy levels became gradually more like the public they serve, a culture was inbred and assimilated because of similar life occurrences. After systems failed for entire decades, it was the failures of trying to improve a section of American society that brought detrimental reformist results.

The end of Nixon ... was the start of the "Me Generation."
Me generation....It is: "what you can do for me?"
It creates an aura that everyone is justified in their attitude, What's in it for Me?

112

Getting it in a hurry, the NY minute is ever present, and Americans think that they are too good for a normal, laid back lifestyle.

"America owes me more."
Another plague that entitlements created
and, the 1970s reinforced.

At the end of President Nixon's administration, America became increasingly suspicious of the war as it dragged on for most of a decade. The following were typical descriptions of what disillusion was like in the 1970s:

Richard Nixon, the 37th President of the United States, is often a controversial figure in American history. While his presidency is marred by the Watergate scandal and other issues, there were several positive contributions and values he embraced during his time in office. Here are some of Nixon's notable good values and achievements:

Environmental Protection:
Nixon was instrumental in the establishment of the Environmental Protection Agency (EPA) in 1970. This agency was created to address growing concerns about pollution and environmental degradation.
He signed into law several key environmental regulations, including the Clean Air Act (1970) and the Clean Water Act (1972), which laid the groundwork for modern environmental protection efforts.
Opening Relations with China:
One of Nixon's most significant achievements was his diplomatic outreach to China, culminating in his 1972 visit to the country. This move helped to normalize relations between the U.S. and China, paving the way for increased trade and international cooperation.

Détente with the Soviet Union:

Nixon pursued a policy of détente, aimed at easing Cold War tensions with the Soviet Union. This included significant arms control agreements such as the Strategic Arms Limitation Talks (SALT I) and the Anti-Ballistic Missile Treaty.

Health and Economic Initiatives:

Nixon advocated for and signed several important health care and social welfare programs, including the establishment of the Occupational Safety and Health Administration (OSHA) to protect workers' rights and safety. He also introduced healthcare reforms, including expanded access to Medicare and Medicaid.

Support for Civil Rights:

Nixon's administration took steps to further civil rights initiatives, including the enforcement of desegregation in schools and promoting affirmative action to address racial inequalities. He created the Office of Minority Business Enterprise to encourage the growth of minority-owned businesses.

Economic Policies:

Nixon implemented various economic policies, including wage and price controls in an attempt to curb inflation and stabilize the economy during a tumultuous period.

Advocacy for Law and Order:

Nixon emphasized the importance of law and order during a time of social upheaval in the 1960s and early 1970s, reflecting a value placed on public safety and stability, although the implementation of these policies often led to criticism regarding civil liberties.

While Nixon's presidency is often overshadowed by scandal and controversy, his administration also made substantive contributions to various areas, including the environment, foreign policy, health care, and civil rights. Evaluating his legacy involves recognizing both the positive outcomes of his policies.

<u>What does it mean if someone is disillusioned?</u>
We have lost faith or trust in something formerly regarded as good or valuable.
The loss of the Vietnam War and the North Vietnamese taking over control of the entire country brought America a feeling of incapability to complete a national task.

Disillusioned 1950s and 1960s lifestyles are fading in America at this time. It is changing more rapidly than at any other time in American history.

People see the rise in two different societies in America, the privileged and the underclass.

The Nixon war was an abhorrent war at home because it was so unpopular with most disillusioned American youth. America's youth thought this was a conflict that only helped the military establishment gain power and control. The War Powers Act ended the war legally. The War Powers Resolution of 1973 (also known as the War Powers Act) "is a congressional resolution designed to limit the U.S. president's ability to initiate (or escalate) military actions abroad." As part of our system of governmental "checks and balances," the law aims to check the executive branch's power when fighting endless wars. It was proven in the war with Iraq to do its job in finalizing the result.

During his administration, President Nixon also took us off the Gold Standard Currency market and started the Federal Reserve. The Federal Reserve started us towards non-stop inflationary times because the Reserve didn't create value, it told everyone what our currency was valued at. They unilaterally changed the world's banking system. Remembering his speech, this move was to make the rest of the world more equal to our dollar's strength. Our dollar did exactly that and fell to equalized other currency levels, so different countries around the world could purchase our products such as steel and automobiles. The problem with that is the fuel deficient economy, American vehicles were not similar to those high MPG vehicles from Japan and Europe. Devaluation was meant to increase exports, close trade deficits, and also shrink the interest payments on borrowed money that our government causally makes in its mode of operation.

It looks as though our economy is moving towards this once again. When our government needs money try print it. Which makes our economy inflationary for all of us.

In the 1970s, the United States experienced significant economic challenges, including high inflation, rising unemployment, and stagnant economic growth, a phenomenon often referred to as "stagflation." During this period, the government's approach to managing the economy and its monetary policy had notable implications.

Monetary Policy and Inflation: In the early 1970s, the U.S. government, under President Richard Nixon, implemented policies that included wage and price controls in an attempt to combat inflation. However, these measures were not effective in the long term. The Federal Reserve also faced pressure to maintain low interest rates to support economic growth, which contributed to an increase in the money supply.

End of the Gold Standard: In 1971, Nixon announced the suspension of the dollar's convertibility into gold, effectively ending the *Bretton Woods system.* This move allowed the U.S. to print more money without the constraint of gold reserves, leading to an increase in the money supply. While this provided short-term relief, it also contributed to rising inflation.

Inflation Rates: Throughout the 1970s, inflation rates soared, peaking at over 13% in 1980. The increase in the money supply, combined with oil price shocks (notably the 1973 oil crisis), contributed to this inflationary environment. The government's ability to print money without immediate consequences led to a loss of confidence in the dollar.

Federal Reserve Response: In response to the persistent inflation, the Federal Reserve, under Chairman Paul Volcker, adopted a more aggressive monetary policy in the late 1970s and early 1980s. This included raising interest rates significantly to curb inflation, which eventually led to a recession but ultimately helped stabilize the economy.

Long-Term Consequences: The economic policies of the 1970s, including the reliance on printing money and the abandonment of the gold standard, had lasting effects on U.S. monetary policy and economic theory. The experience of stagflation challenged traditional economic thinking and led to a reevaluation of monetary policy approaches.

In summary, the 1970s were marked by significant economic turmoil, and the government's approach to managing money supply and inflation had profound implications for the U.S. economy. The lessons learned from this period continue to influence economic policy today.

The Bretton Woods system was a monetary order established in July 1944 during a conference held in Bretton Woods, New Hampshire, attended by representatives from 44 countries. The system aimed to create a stable international monetary framework in the aftermath of World War II and to promote economic cooperation and reconstruction.

Here are the key features and implications of the Bretton Woods system:

Fixed Exchange Rates: Under the Bretton Woods system, countries agreed to peg their currencies to the U.S. dollar, which was in turn convertible to gold at a fixed rate of $35 per ounce. This created a system of fixed exchange rates, where currencies would fluctuate only within a narrow band.

U.S. Dollar as the Reserve Currency: The U.S. dollar became the primary reserve currency for international trade and finance. This was largely due to the United States' economic strength and its significant gold reserves at the time.

International Monetary Fund (IMF): The Bretton Woods conference led to the creation of the IMF, which was established to oversee the international monetary system, provide financial assistance to countries facing balance of payments problems, and promote exchange rate stability.

World Bank: The conference also established the International Bank for Reconstruction and Development (IBRD), commonly known as the World Bank, to provide financial and technical assistance for post-war reconstruction and development projects.

Implications:

Economic Stability: The Bretton Woods system contributed to a period of relative economic stability and growth in the post-war era, facilitating international trade and investment.

Trade Expansion: By providing a stable exchange rate environment, the system encouraged countries to engage in international trade, leading to increased economic interdependence.

Challenges and Strain: Over time, the fixed exchange rate system faced challenges, including inflation in the U.S., trade imbalances, and the growing demand for dollars. As countries accumulated dollar reserves, concerns about the sustainability of the U.S. dollar's convertibility into gold grew.

Collapse of the System: The Bretton Woods system began to unravel in the late 1960s and early 1970s, culminating in President Richard Nixon's decision in 1971 to suspend the dollar's convertibility into gold, effectively ending the Bretton Woods system. This event is often referred to as the "Nixon Shock."

Transition to Floating Exchange Rates: After the collapse of the Bretton Woods system, many countries transitioned to a system of floating exchange rates, where currency values are determined by market forces rather than fixed pegs.

Legacy:
The Bretton Woods system laid the groundwork for modern international monetary relations and institutions. The IMF and World Bank continue to play significant roles in global economic governance, and the lessons learned from the Bretton Woods era continue to inform discussions about international monetary policy and economic cooperation.

No good news here....
The oil embargo of the early 70s was a driving force in keeping Americans in a constant malaise. In 1973 and 1974 the lines of backed up cars waited to get their allotment of fuel to get back and forth to work. People commonly waited in lines longer than their commute to work. The shortage was man made and meant to destroy the American lifestyle. It were these oil barrens that crippled America for years. It was not until strong military forces of America were called upon to protect these oil rich countries from one another that the flow of oil was released. At such a precious cost to America, the world saw that simply turning off the spigot of oil supplied to an industrious nation surely beget another, and another, extortion of America. These years were soon to be known as the Malaise Era in America.

The oil embargo of the early 1970s, particularly the 1973 oil crisis, had a profound impact on the U.S. economy and contributed to a period of economic malaise characterized by stagflation—simultaneous high inflation and unemployment.
Background of the Oil Embargo
OPEC Formation: The Organization of the Petroleum Exporting Countries (OPEC) was formed in 1960, but it gained significant power in the early 1970s. In October 1973, OPEC members, particularly Arab nations, imposed an oil embargo on countries that supported Israel during the Yom Kippur War, including the United States.
Oil Price Shock: The embargo led to a dramatic increase in oil prices, with the price of crude oil quadrupling in a short

period. This sudden spike in energy costs had widespread repercussions for economies dependent on oil.

The period from the 1970s to the 1990s saw significant fluctuations in gas prices in the United States influenced by various economic, geopolitical, and market factors these are the key events and trends during this time:

1970s:
Oil Embargo (1973-1974): The 1973 oil crisis, triggered by the OPEC oil embargo, led to a dramatic increase in oil prices. Gas prices in the U.S. rose sharply, with the average price per gallon increasing from about 39 cents in 1973 to over 55 cents by 1974. This period marked the beginning of a sustained increase in fuel prices.

Second Oil Shock (1979): The Iranian Revolution in 1979 caused another spike in oil prices, leading to further increases in gas prices. By the end of the decade, average gas prices had risen to around $1.20 per gallon.

1980s:
Volatile Prices: The early 1980s saw continued volatility in oil prices due to geopolitical tensions and changes in OPEC production levels. Gas prices fluctuated, but by the mid-1980s, prices began to stabilize and even decline.

Price Decline: By 1986, oil prices fell significantly due to a combination of increased production from non-OPEC countries and a decrease in demand. Gas prices dropped to around 89 cents per gallon by the end of the decade.

1990s
Gulf War (1990-1991): The invasion of Kuwait by Iraq in 1990 led to concerns about oil supply disruptions, causing a spike in oil prices. Gas prices rose again, reaching around $1.20 per gallon during the early 1991 conflict.

Post-Gulf War Stability: After the Gulf War, oil prices stabilized, and gas prices generally remained lower throughout much of the 1990s. By the mid-1990s, average gas prices were around $1.10 to $1.30 per gallon.

Late 1990s Trends: Towards the end of the decade, gas prices began to rise again due to increasing global demand, particularly from emerging economies, and production cuts by OPEC. By 1999, prices were approaching $1.50 per gallon.

Overall, the period from the 1970s to the 1990s was marked by significant fluctuations in gas prices, driven by geopolitical events, changes in oil production, and shifts in global demand.

Economic Impact:

Inflation: The sharp rise in oil prices contributed to inflation, as the cost of energy affected the prices of goods and services across the economy. Higher transportation and production costs were passed on to consumers, leading to increased prices.

Stagflation: The combination of rising prices and stagnant economic growth resulted in stagflation, a term that became widely used during this period. Unemployment rates rose as businesses struggled with higher costs and reduced consumer spending.

Shift in Energy Policy: In response to the crisis, the U.S. government began to focus on energy conservation, alternative energy sources, and reducing dependence on foreign oil. This included initiatives to promote fuel efficiency in vehicles and investments in renewable energy research.

Long-Term Effects:

Economic Malaise: The oil crisis contributed to a prolonged period of economic malaise in the U.S. during the 1970s, characterized by low growth, high inflation, and rising unemployment. This period of uncertainty affected consumer confidence and investment.

Geopolitical Implications: The oil embargo also had significant geopolitical implications, leading to shifts in U.S. foreign policy and relationships with oil-producing nations. It underscored the importance of energy security in international relations.

Legacy of the 1970s: The economic challenges of the 1970s influenced subsequent economic policies and debates about energy independence, inflation control, and the role of government in managing the economy. The lessons learned from this period continue to resonate in discussions about energy policy and economic resilience today.

The oil embargo of the early 1970s was indeed a driving force behind the economic malaise experienced in the United States during that decade, contributing to inflation, unemployment, and a reevaluation of energy policies.

From 1973 to 1974 the S&P 500 fell into a
*40% lost **Bear** Market*
that took five years to get out of.

The Carter doctrine led America to protect and defend the same (OPEC) countries that until recently were rubbing our noses into the fact they controlled the flow of oil (and its cost to us) and that became a weapon to crush our US economy. The **"Malaise Era"** refers to the U.S. ***President Jimmy Carter's*** dereliction and relinquishing – he described it this way: "we are living in an illusion, you have to break out of it. While it may feel jarred at first, this is normal as you come to terms with reality."

The 1970s also saw the European attitude of "I deserve so much more" (starting with a Mercedes in every driveway) than my neighbors is seen everywhere in America. It is a time when Women's Rights were summarily dropped, and this era of "Me" took over all aspects of one's self-approval in life. This disillusionment of an entire class of Americans became increasingly narcissistic and less empathetic than any other generation prior. A new American attitude arose in the mid-1970s. Lost was the communitarian-ism found across American youth communities that prevailed in the 1960s.

The "Me" generation lifestyle became a clear contrast with the intertwining social values prevalent in the United States.

The 1960s adolescent genesis, which made it through the end of another war, surmised that they ended the latest government-advocated crusade, therefore, they should be treated better because their protesting ended the war. The 1970s and 80s were the time this assemblage of American society harvested their rightful acknowledgeable. The disillusionment of a lost war halfway across the world was forgotten, and the American pride and spirit internalized within the new **Me Generation**.

The term "Me Generation" refers to a cultural phenomenon that emerged in the United States during the 1970s, characterized by a focus on individualism, self-expression, and personal fulfillment. It is often associated with the baby boomer generation, particularly those who came of age during this time. Here are some key aspects of the Me Generation and its implications for American society:

Me Gen Characteristics:

Individualism: The Me Generation emphasized personal identity and self-discovery. Many individuals sought to prioritize their own needs, desires, and aspirations over traditional societal expectations or communal responsibilities.

Self-Expression: This era saw a rise in various forms of self-expression, including art, music, fashion, and lifestyle choices. The counterculture movements of the 1960s, which advocated for peace, love, and social change, laid the groundwork for this focus on personal expression.

Consumerism: The Me Generation coincided with a period of economic prosperity in the U.S., leading to increased consumerism. Many individuals sought to acquire goods and experiences that reflected their personal identities, contributing to a culture of consumption.

Psychological Exploration: There was a growing interest in psychology, self-help, and personal development during this time. Concepts such as self-actualization and personal growth became popular, influenced by figures like Abraham Maslow and the humanistic psychology movement.

Rejection of Traditional Norms: Many members of the Me Generation questioned or rejected traditional values and norms, including those related to family, career, and social roles. This included a rise in alternative lifestyles, such as communal living and non-traditional family structures.

Implications for American Society Cultural Shifts: The Me Generation contributed to significant cultural shifts in American society, including changes in attitudes toward gender roles, sexuality, and family structures. The feminist movement gained momentum during this time, advocating for women's rights and equality.

Impact on Politics: The focus on individual rights and personal freedom influenced political discourse and activism. Issues such as civil rights, environmentalism, and LGBTQ+ rights gained prominence as individuals sought to assert their identities and advocate for social change.

Criticism and Backlash: The Me Generation faced criticism for perceived selfishness and a lack of social responsibility. Some commentators argued that the emphasis on individualism led to a decline in community engagement and a sense of social cohesion.

Legacy: The values and attitudes of the Me Generation have had a lasting impact on American culture. The emphasis on self-expression and personal fulfillment continues to resonate in contemporary society, influencing everything from social media to consumer behavior.

The Me Generation represented a *significant cultural shift* in the United States during the 1970s, emphasizing individualism, self-expression, and personal fulfillment. While it brought about positive changes in terms of social progress and cultural diversity, it also faced criticism for fostering a sense of selfishness and detachment from community values. The legacy of the Me Generation continues to shape American society today.

Chapter Four:

Medias narrative shapes our
Nation's Malaise.

*Cynicism in the US is rising, and the media is contributing to
the country's current malaise, from the 1960s to the present.*

Starting with:
The Media set the stage for Americans daily, defining this
National Malaise and the rise of cynicism in post 1960s
America through the evening news.

American society has seen tremendous change from the
1960s to the present, frequently coupled with a generalized
sense of social unease, discontent, and a feeling that something fundamental about the country is wrong. Often called
"national malaise," this phenomenon represents a wide
range of concerns, from social unrest and economic instability to a loss of faith in national ideals and the direction of
progress. National malaise is not static; its main causes and
traits have probably changed over time. Economic factors
like high inflation and energy crises, for example, greatly
influenced the 1970s' sense of malaise, whereas later eras
may have attributed this uneasiness to other factors like
political polarization, social divisions, or the effects of world
events. A thorough analysis requires an understanding of the
subtleties of national malaise in each era.

A significant rise in public cynicism, which is typified by widespread mistrust of organizations like the government, media, and businesses as well as mistrust of leaders and their
hidden agendas, has added to this unease. Cynicism can
take many forms, such as disengagement from civic life and
the widespread perception that constructive social change is
unlikely or impossible. It is crucial to understand that cynicism can develop as a reaction to objective facts, like cases

of corporate wrongdoing or government corruption, as well as as a result of media framing that continuously highlights negativity and encourages mistrust. Being able to differentiate between healthy skepticism—which is necessary for a functioning democracy—and more destructive, crippling cynicism is necessary for a nuanced understanding of the current sociopolitical landscape.

This study intends to investigate the complex interplay between media narratives and the formation of public opinion, with a particular emphasis on how, from the 1960s to the present, these narratives have mirrored and possibly intensified a feeling of national gloom and heightened cynicism in the US. To provide a thorough overview, the analysis will take an interdisciplinary approach, referencing sociology, political science, media studies, and historical analysis. Furthermore, the report will consider the significant role of evolving media technologies in shaping the dissemination and impact of narratives related to national malaise and cynicism, recognizing that the way information is consumed and shared has undergone radical transformations over the past six decades.

Seeds of Discontent and the Emergence of the "Living Room War" during the turbulent 1960s.

A crucial decade in American history, the 1960s saw significant social, political, and cultural changes that prepared the way for many of the societal trends seen in later decades. During this time, serious challenges to the established social order emerged, undermining the high levels of national confidence that defined the years following World War II.

Major Historical Events and the Initial Cracks in National Confidence.

The Civil Rights Movement stands as a defining feature of the 1960s, bringing to the forefront the long-standing struggle for racial equality and exposing deep-seated societal divisions. Events such as the Greensboro sit-ins in 1960, the Freedom Rides beginning in 1961, and the March on Washington in 1963 highlighted the pervasive racial inequalities and the often brutal resistance faced by those advocating for change. While these events ultimately led to landmark legislation like the Civil Rights Act of 1964 and the Voting Rights Act of 1965 , they also revealed a nation grappling with fundamental issues of justice and equality, potentially contributing to a sense of unease among various segments of the population.

The Vietnam War also escalated dramatically throughout the 1960s, becoming a major source of national division and disillusionment. The initial deployment of U.S. combat troops in 1965 marked a significant turning point, leading to increasing casualties and a growing anti-war movement within the United States. The perceived lack of clear objectives, coupled with the graphic realities of the war brought into American homes via television, signaled a significant challenge to national confidence and trust in the government's handling of the conflict.

The Assassination of President John F. Kennedy in November 1963 sent shock waves through the nation, leaving a profound sense of shock and trauma. The sudden loss of a young and charismatic leader, coupled with the subsequent investigations and the emergence of various conspiracy theories , likely contributed to a growing sense of instability and a questioning of established narratives and institutions.

Furthermore, the 1960s witnessed significant Social and Cultural Upheaval, most notably the rise of the counterculture movement. This movement, largely driven by young people, represented a rejection of mainstream values, norms, and authorities, reflecting a growing dissatisfaction with the status quo among a significant portion of the population.

Media Narratives of the Civil Rights Movement: Unveiling Societal Divisions and Government Response.

In the early years of the Civil Rights Movement, national print media displayed a reluctance to provide adequate coverage, keeping the struggle largely at a local level. However, as the movement gained momentum and events became increasingly newsworthy, national media attention grew, bringing to light the brutal conditions faced by African Americans, particularly in the southern United States. The visual power of television played a crucial role, with images of peaceful demonstrators being met with violence from police and white mobs sparking outrage across the nation. These images, such as those from the sit-in movement in Greensboro and Montgomery, where protesters were attacked while authorities stood by , helped to galvanize support for the movement and exposed the stark societal divisions along racial lines.

Media coverage also documented the varied responses from government entities, ranging from legislative support for civil rights to active resistance and even complicity in suppressing the movement. For instance, the arrest of Martin Luther King Jr. on what were described as "phony charges" of tax evasion illustrated the use of government power to target and undermine the movement's leadership. The libel suits filed by Alabama officials against the New York Times following an ad placed by civil rights activists detailing an "unprecedented wave of terror" further exemplified attempts to stifle critical voices and protect the status quo of segregation. It is also important to acknowledge the vital role of the Black Press during this era, which served as a crucial source of protest against racial inequality and provided news and information for the Black community, often offering perspectives distinct from the mainstream media. The media's framing of the Civil Rights Movement, while essential for raising national awareness and fostering support for change, also likely contributed to a sense of national unease by starkly revealing deep-seated injustices and societal conflicts. The focus on violence, discrimination, and instances of government inaction could have eroded trust in institutions for many Americans.

The Vietnam War as a Televised Conflict: Shifting Public Opinion and Eroding Trust.

The Vietnam War is often referred to as the "first television war," and this unprecedented level of visual coverage had a profound impact on public opinion. For the first time in American history, graphic images and reports from the front lines were brought directly into people's living rooms, offering a stark and often brutal portrayal of the conflict. This direct exposure to the realities of war led to a significant shift in public sentiment compared to previous conflicts, where news coverage was often more controlled and focused on positive aspects of the war effort.

Early media reporting on the Vietnam War often aligned with the government's narrative, portraying the conflict as a necessary defense against communist aggression. However, as the war dragged on, and reports from journalists on the ground increasingly contradicted official accounts of progress and success, media skepticism grew. This shift towards more critical reporting likely fueled a growing sense of public disillusionment and eroded trust in the government's handling of the war. A significant turning point in media coverage came after the *Tet Offensive* in early 1968. Walter Cronkite, the highly respected anchor of the CBS Evening News, traveled to Vietnam and, upon his return, delivered an editorial stating his belief that the war was "mired in stalemate". This influential shift in reporting from "the most trusted man in America" is widely seen as a key moment in the decline of public support for the war. Unlike previous wars, the Vietnam War era saw a relative lack of government censorship on the press. This allowed journalists to report on the realities of the war more freely, including the increasing casualties and the questionable justifications for continued involvement, which contrasted sharply with the often-optimistic official narratives emanating from Washington. The constant exposure to the human cost of the war, coupled with the growing skepticism in media reporting, played a crucial role in shaping public perception and fostering a sense of national malaise and distrust in the government's leadership.

Popular Culture in the 1960s: Reflecting and Amplifying Social Unrest.

Popular culture in the 1960s served as a powerful lens through which the social and political turmoil of the decade was both reflected and amplified. Music became a significant voice for protest and social commentary, with artists addressing issues such as the Vietnam War, the Civil Rights Movement, and broader social inequalities. Songs like Buffalo Springfield's "For What It's Worth," initially about protests against a curfew, became anthems for the anti-war movement. Edwin Starr's "War (What is it good for?)" directly confronted the Vietnam conflict and resonated deeply with a public increasingly questioning the war. This music resonated particularly with young people, who formed a significant part of the counterculture, and amplified feelings of discontent and a desire for change.

While direct depictions of the Vietnam War in film and television were somewhat limited during the 1960s, many productions indirectly addressed the anxieties and divisions of the era. Films like Bonnie and Clyde and M*A*S*H (though set in the Korean War) reflected a growing cynicism towards authority and societal norms. Television shows, while generally more cautious, began to touch upon social issues, albeit often indirectly. The hippie counterculture's rejection of mainstream norms was visibly expressed through fashion, art, and lifestyle. Long hair, colorful clothing, and the embrace of alternative spiritualities and lifestyles signaled a significant level of dissatisfaction with traditional American society. The Woodstock music festival in 1969 became a powerful symbol of this countercultural movement, representing a desire for peace, love, and a rejection of the established order. Popular culture in the 1960s, therefore, acted as both a mirror reflecting the social and political turmoil and a catalyst amplifying feelings of unrest and contributing to a sense that traditional norms and institutions were being challenged at a fundamental level. The widespread embrace of countercultural expressions indicated that a significant segment of the population felt alienated from or critical of mainstream American life, further contributing to the growing sense of national unease.

Early Public Opinion Data: Tracking Initial Declines in Trust and National Sentiment.

Public opinion data from the 1960s provides quantitative evidence of a significant shift in national sentiment, particularly a marked decline in trust in the federal government. Polls conducted by the University of Michigan, starting in 1958, revealed that in the early 1960s, more than 70% of Americans expressed confidence in the federal government, peaking at 76% in 1964. However, this high level of trust began a sharp downward slide in the mid-1960s. This erosion of trust coincided with the escalation of the Vietnam War, the growing visibility of the Civil Rights Movement and its associated unrest, and the assassination of President Kennedy. By the late 1960s, trust in government had fallen considerably, reflecting the impact of these major events and the accompanying media narratives on public perceptions.

Furthermore, the mid-1960s also saw a shift in how Americans viewed the role of government. For the first time in 1965, more people indicated that "big government" posed a greater threat to the future than "big labor". This sentiment reflected a growing concern about the size and scope of the federal government, particularly with the expansion of social programs under President Johnson's Great Society. While these programs aimed to address poverty and inequality, they also led to debates about government overreach and efficiency, potentially contributing to a sense of unease and distrust among some segments of the population. The initial high levels of trust in the early 1960s, followed by a significant drop by the end of the decade, strongly suggest that the events and media coverage of this tumultuous period had a profound impact on shaping public sentiment, leading to a notable decline in confidence in the nation's institutions.

The 1970s: The "Malaise Era" and the Crisis of Confidence.

The 1970s are often remembered as a period of significant national malaise, characterized by a confluence of political scandals, economic instability, and a lingering sense of disillusionment following the Vietnam War. This era witnessed a deepening of the cracks in national confidence that had begun to appear in the previous decade.

Key Events: Watergate, Economic Instability, and the End of the Vietnam War.

The Watergate Scandal, which unfolded throughout the early to mid-1970s, had a profound and lasting impact on public trust in government and political institutions. The break-in at the Democratic National Committee headquarters in 1972 and the subsequent cover-up by the Nixon administration revealed a pattern of deceit and corruption at the highest levels of government. The extensive media coverage of the Watergate hearings and the eventual resignation of President Nixon in 1974 deeply eroded public faith in the presidency and the integrity of the political system.

The 1970s were also marked by significant Economic Instability. The American economy suffered from stagflation, a combination of high inflation and high unemployment, exacerbated by an energy crisis stemming from oil embargoes. The decline of American manufacturing and increased international economic competition further contributed to economic anxieties. These economic challenges created widespread anxiety and significantly contributed to the overall sense of national malaise. The struggles of the U.S. automotive industry during this "Malaise Era" served as a potent symbol of broader economic difficulties.

The End of the Vietnam War in 1975, following the withdrawal of American troops, also left a significant impact on the national psyche. The circumstances surrounding the U.S. withdrawal and the subsequent fall of South Vietnam to communist forces led to a sense of defeat and questioned America's role and capabilities on the world stage, contributing to what was termed the "Vietnam malaise".

Furthermore, the 1970s saw various Social and Cultural Shifts that contributed to the sense of national unease. Rising crime rates, increased drug use, and changing social norms related to sexuality and family structures led to concerns about "decaying morality". These social anxieties, coupled with the political and economic turmoil, created a pervasive feeling that the nation was facing a period of decline.

Media Coverage of Political Scandals and Economic Hardship: Deepening Public Cynicism.

The Watergate scandal dominated news coverage throughout much of the 1970s, with extensive reporting on the unfolding revelations of government misconduct. The constant stream of negative information about the President and his administration, including details of illegal activities and attempts to obstruct justice, deeply eroded public trust in the executive branch and the political system as a whole. The media's persistent investigation and reporting on Watergate played a crucial role in bringing these issues to light and holding those in power accountable, but it also contributed to a significant increase in public cynicism towards government.

The economic crisis of the 1970s also received significant media attention, with widespread reporting on inflation, unemployment, and the energy shortage. News narratives often emphasized the hardship faced by ordinary Americans as they struggled with rising prices, job losses, and long lines at gas stations. This constant focus on economic woes likely fueled public anxiety and a sense of national decline, further contributing to a cynical outlook on the nation's future.

The Iran hostage crisis, which began in late 1979, also received extensive media coverage. The prolonged captivity of American diplomats in Iran and the perceived inability of the U.S. government to secure their release led to a sense of national powerlessness and a decline in national prestige. The constant media attention on this crisis further amplified feelings of frustration and cynicism about America's standing in the world. The 1970s, therefore, witnessed a sustained period of negative news coverage, encompassing political scandals, economic hardship, and international setbacks. This constant exposure to negative narratives likely deepened public cynicism and reinforced the prevailing sense of national malaise.

Popular Culture in the 1970s: Mirroring National Anxiety and Disillusionment.

Popular culture in the 1970s often mirrored the national mood of anxiety and disillusionment. Films of the era frequently explored themes of distrust, paranoia, and societal breakdown. Crime dramas and dystopian narratives reflected a growing unease about the state of American society. For example, films like Dirty Harry and Taxi Driver portrayed a gritty and often violent urban landscape, reflecting anxieties about crime and social decay.

Music continued to be a platform for expressing disillusionment and social commentary. While some genres offered escapism, many artists addressed the political and economic realities of the time, often with a tone of cynicism or frustration. Television also reflected the changing social norms and anxieties of the decade. Shows like "All in the Family" broke ground by tackling controversial social and political issues directly, mirroring the debates and tensions within American society. The popularity of such shows indicated a public grappling with complex and often uncomfortable realities.

The themes explored in popular culture during the 1970s, therefore, often aligned with the dominant news narratives of the time, suggesting a reinforcing effect where media and entertainment both reflected and potentially amplified the sense of national malaise and a loss of faith in institutions.

Public Opinion Polls: Documenting a Significant Drop in Trust and a Sense of National Decline.

Public opinion polls from the 1970s provide compelling evidence of a significant decline in public trust and a pervasive sense of national malaise. Trust in the federal government, which had already begun to decline in the late 1960s, bottomed out in the late 1970s, reaching historically low levels. By the end of the decade, only about a quarter of Americans felt that they could trust the government at least most of the time. This dramatic drop in trust underscored the depth of the crisis of confidence during this period, largely attributed to the Watergate scandal and the ongoing economic difficulties.

Furthermore, the decline in confidence wasn't limited to the federal government. Public opinion data revealed a significant erosion of trust across various institutions, both political and nonpolitical, including the press, business, and even religion. This broader decline indicated a widespread societal disillusionment and a questioning of the fundamental pillars of American society. President Jimmy Carter himself acknowledged this prevailing sentiment in his famous "malaise" speech in 1979, where he spoke of a "crisis of confidence" that was gripping the nation. Although he never actually used the word "malaise," the speech resonated with many Americans who felt a deep sense of unease about the direction of the country. The public opinion data from the 1970s, therefore, strongly corroborates the narrative of a nation experiencing a profound crisis of confidence and a significant increase in cynicism, fueled by the political and economic turmoil and the way these were portrayed in the media.

Comparative Analysis of Economic Conditions and Public Sentiment in America during the 1970s: Structured Brainstorm.

To Start:

Putting this in context, an overview of the 1970s would be seen as a decade of economic upheaval (stagflation, energy crises) and shifting public trust (Watergate, post-Vietnam).

My objective to put this in context for you; I explored how economic conditions influenced public sentiment and vice versa, with attention to regional, demographic, and cultural dimensions.

These economic problems of the 1970s were highlighted everyday in the living room nightly in America.

These Indicators are highlighted from Americas boosts with:

- Stagflation (e.g., inflation peaking at 13.3% in 1979, and unemployment rising to 9% in 1975).
- GDP fluctuations (recessions in 1970, 1973–75, and 1980).

Major Events:

- 1973 OPEC oil embargo and 1979 energy crisis.
- End of Bretton Woods (1971) and transition to fiat currency.
- De-industrialization and Rust Belt decline.

Public Sentiment Drivers:
- Political Distrust: Watergate scandal (1974), Carter's "malaise" speech (1979).
- Cultural Expressions: Films (*Taxi Driver*, *Network*), music (punk's anger, disco escapism).
- Elections and Protests: Tax revolts (Proposition 13, 1978), rise of neo-liberalism, pre-Reagan.

Comparative Analysis Framework
- Temporal Comparison
  - Early 1970s (Nixon's wage-price controls vs. public skepticism).
  - Mid-1970s (post-oil crisis recession and consumer pessimism).
  - Late 1970s (Carter's policies and the "misery index").
- Regional Divergence:
  - Rust Belt (job losses, union strikes) vs. Sun Belt (growth, suburbanization).
- Demographic Groups:
  White-collar professionals (relative stability) contrast with blue-collar workers (discontent).

Racial differences in the impact of Inflation and Unemployment.

- Policy Responses:
  The way the public viewed Nixon's and Carter's economic policies.
  - Shift from Keynesianism to monetarism (Federal Reserve's Volcker Shock).

Case Studies
- 1973 Oil Crisis: Gas shortages, inflation spikes, and consumer anger.
- 1979 Energy Crisis: Synced with Carter's approval drop and Reagan's rise.

- 1977 NYC Blackout: Symbolic of systemic fragility and urban anxiety.

Cultural and Political Responses: - Media Role: TV news (such as nightly inflation reports) exacerbates economic anxiety.
- Labor Movements: Strikes (e.g., 1970 U.S. Postal strike) as barometers of frustration.
- Electoral Shifts: Reagan's landslide victory in 1980 reflected the desire for economic reform.

Methodological Considerations:
- Data Sources: FRED for economic metrics; Gallup polls for sentiment.
- Challenges: Disentangling economic vs. political factors (e.g., Watergate's impact on trust).

Conclusion:
Economic difficulties (unemployment, stagflation) undermined institutional trust, which stoked cultural pessimism and political realignment. The primary conclusions were these:
- Legacy: 1970s crises paved the way for neo-liberal reforms and reshaped partisan loyalties.
- Modern Parallels: Lessons for understanding economic-politico feedback loops (e.g., post-2008 populism).
Potential Sources for Further Research
- Primary: FRED datasets, Gallup archives, presidential speeches, *The New York Times* archives.
- Secondary: Bruce Schulman's *The Seventies*, Jefferson Cowie's *Stayin' Alive* (labor history), documentaries (*The Seventies* CNN series).

Through demographic, temporal, and thematic lenses, this framework methodically connects economic data to public sentiment, providing a nuanced examination of a decade that was revolutionary.

The 1980s and 1990s: Shifting Narratives in a Changing Media Landscape.

The decades of the 1980s and 1990s brought significant shifts in the American landscape, marked by a sense of renewed optimism for some, the end of the Cold War, and the emergence of new social and political challenges. These changes were reflected in evolving media narratives within a rapidly transforming media environment.

Major Events: The Reagan Era, the End of the Cold War, and Emerging Social Issues.

The election of Ronald Reagan in 1980 ushered in an era often associated with a sense of renewed optimism, particularly regarding the economy and national strength. Reagan's conservative policies and his emphasis on American exceptionalism resonated with many voters who felt that the nation had lost its way during the 1970s. The economic recovery that occurred during the Reagan years further contributed to this sense of optimism for some segments of the population.

The end of the Cold War in the early 1990s marked a monumental shift in global politics. The collapse of the Soviet Union and the dismantling of the Iron Curtain were widely seen as a victory for the United States and its democratic ideals. This event led to discussions about a "peace dividend" and America's role in a newly unipolar world.

However, these decades also saw the emergence and intensification of significant social issues. The AIDS epidemic, which gained prominence in the 1980s , became a major public health crisis and a source of fear and stigma. The "culture wars" over issues like abortion, religion in schools, and LGBTQ+ rights intensified, reflecting deep societal divisions. Furthermore, economic inequality continued to rise, creating concerns about social justice and the American dream.

Political scandals also continued to surface during the 1980s and 1990s. The Iran-Contra affair during the Reagan administration and the impeachment of President Bill Clinton in the late 1990s raised ethical concerns and potentially undermined public trust in political leaders.

A significant development during this period was the rise of the Internet and early forms of on-line communication. While still in its nascent stages for much of this time, the Internet began to change the media landscape, offering new ways for people to access information and communicate with each other, although its full impact on public perception would become more apparent in the following decades.

Media Narratives: From Renewed Optimism to Lingering Concerns:
Media narratives in the 1980s often initially reflected the optimism associated with the Reagan era and its economic policies. Coverage of the end of the Cold War was largely positive, often framed as a triumph for American values and an opportunity for global peace. The narrative of a "peace dividend," suggesting that reduced military spending could be redirected to domestic needs, gained traction in media discussions.

However, media attention also increasingly focused on emerging social issues. The AIDS epidemic received significant coverage, often highlighting the devastating human cost and the challenges in addressing the crisis. Reports on rising economic inequality raised concerns about the widening gap between the rich and the poor and its implications for social mobility and the American dream. Political scandals, such as Iran-Contra and the Clinton impeachment, continued to be major news stories, often framed in ways that emphasized the erosion of trust and ethical lapses in leadership. Therefore, the media narratives of the 1980s and 1990s were more complex than a simple return to optimism. While the end of the Cold War provided a positive overarching narrative, persistent social issues and recurring political scandals continued to fuel cynicism and raise concerns about the state of the nation for many Americans.

The Rise of 24-Hour News and its Impact on Narrative Dissemination:

A significant development in the media landscape during the 1980s was the launch of CNN in 1980. This marked a shift towards a continuous 24-hour news cycle, a departure from the traditional model of scheduled news broadcasts. The advent of 24-hour news dramatically increased the volume and speed of news dissemination. The constant need for content in this new environment potentially led to an increased focus on immediate events and breaking news, sometimes at the expense of more in-depth analysis and contextualization.

While partisan news outlets became more prominent later, the rise of 24-hour news created a space for different perspectives and voices to emerge, although this also laid the groundwork for a more fragmented media environment. The constant flow of information, while offering greater access to news, could also potentially amplify both positive and negative narratives, depending on the framing and focus of the news coverage. The pressure to attract and retain viewers in a competitive 24-hour market might have also incentivized a focus on conflict and negativity, as these tend to be more attention-grabbing, potentially contributing to a gradual increase in public cynicism over time.

Public Sentiment; Fluctuations and the Persistence of Cynicism:

Public sentiment during the 1980s and 1990s showed some fluctuations. The Reagan years saw an initial rise in trust in government among some segments of the population, likely fueled by the economic recovery and a sense of renewed national pride. However, this initial increase did not necessarily translate into a long-term reversal of the cynicism that had taken hold in the 1970s. Throughout the 1990s, despite a period of economic prosperity for many, public trust in government and other institutions continued to erode. Political scandals, such as the Clinton impeachment, likely contributed to this continued decline in trust.

The underlying trend of increasing cynicism, therefore, seemed to persist throughout the 1980s and 1990s, suggesting that deeper societal factors were at play beyond specific political administrations or economic conditions. While specific events and media narratives could influence public mood in the short term, a more fundamental erosion of trust in institutions appeared to be taking place. The contrast between periods of economic improvement and the continued decline in trust suggests that factors beyond economic well-being, possibly including media narratives around social issues and political scandals, were contributing to this persistent cynicism.

The 2000s and 2010s: The Digital Age and the Intensification of Cynicism:
The dawn of the 21st century and the subsequent decades have been characterized by trans-formative events and the pervasive influence of the digital age. This period has witnessed a further intensification of public cynicism, shaped by major national crises and a rapidly evolving media landscape.

Key Events: 9/11, the Wars in Afghanistan and Iraq, the Great Recession, and the Rise of Social Media:
The terrorist attacks of September 11th, 2001, had a profound and immediate impact on American society, initially fostering a strong sense of national unity and a surge in trust in government as the nation responded to the crisis. However, this unity proved to be relatively short-lived.

The subsequent Wars in Afghanistan and Iraq, launched in response to the 9/11 attacks, became protracted conflicts with significant human and financial costs. As these wars dragged on, and controversies arose regarding their justifications and conduct, public disillusionment grew, leading to a decline in trust in the government's foreign policy decisions and overall national morale.

The Great Recession of 2008 had a devastating impact on the American economy and the lives of millions of people. The collapse of the housing market, the failures of major financial institutions, and the ensuing economic hardship led to a significant erosion of public trust in financial institutions and the government's ability to regulate the economy effectively.

This period also witnessed the rapid rise of Social Media Platforms, which fundamentally transformed communication and information sharing. Platforms like Facebook and Twitter became dominant forces in how people consumed and shared news and opinions, creating new avenues for narratives to spread and influence public perception.

The 2000s and 2010s were also marked by Increasing Political Polarization and Social Divisions. Deep ideological divides, often amplified by media narratives, led to greater animosity between different political groups and a decline in civility in public discourse.

Widespread discontent with the status quo was also reflected in the emergence of social movements like the Occupy Wall Street movement in 2011, which protested economic inequality , and the Black Lives Matter movement, which gained prominence in the mid-2010s to protest racial injustice and police brutality. These movements highlighted deep-seated grievances and a continued sense of national malaise for many Americans.

Media Narratives in the Age of Instant Information and Polarization:

Following the initial surge of patriotic narratives after the 9/11 attacks, media coverage of the Wars in Afghanistan and Iraq gradually became more critical. As the wars continued without clear end in sight and the human and financial costs mounted, media narratives increasingly questioned the strategic goals and the overall effectiveness of the military interventions.

The Great Recession of 2008 received intense media scrutiny, with extensive coverage of its causes and consequences. Media narratives often framed the crisis as a failure of the financial system and inadequate government regulation, potentially fueling public anger and distrust towards both financial institutions and government entities.

The media landscape of the 2000s and 2010s was also characterized by the increasing prominence of partisan media outlets. The rise of cable news channels with openly partisan leanings and the proliferation of politically oriented websites and blogs contributed to a more fragmented and polarized media environment. These partisan outlets often presented narratives that reinforced existing biases and contributed to the growing ideological divide in the country.

The Role of Social Media in Shaping Public Discourse and Amplifying Division.

Social media platforms emerged as a dominant force in shaping public discourse during the 2000s and 2010s. These platforms provided avenues for citizen journalism and the dissemination of alternative narratives that sometimes challenged mainstream media accounts. Social media played a crucial role in organizing and amplifying social movements like Occupy Wall Street and Black Lives Matter, allowing for the rapid spread of information and the mobilization of large numbers of people to protest against economic inequality and racial injustice.

However, the rise of social media also brought significant challenges. The spread of misinformation and "fake news" became a major concern, eroding trust in traditional media and other institutions. The decentralized nature of these platforms made it difficult to control the flow of false or misleading information, contributing to a more fragmented and distrustful information environment. Furthermore, social media algorithms often create echo chambers and filter bubbles, reinforcing existing biases by showing users content they are likely to agree with and limiting their exposure to diverse perspectives. This phenomenon can exacerbate political polarization and contribute to increased cynicism towards opposing viewpoints.

Public Opinion Data: Deepening Mistrust in Institutions and Increasing Polarization:
Public opinion data from the 2000s and 2010s reflects a continued decline in trust in government and other institutions, reaching historically low levels. Surveys consistently showed that fewer than three-in-ten Americans expressed trust in the federal government for much of this period. This deepening crisis of trust extended beyond government to include media, business, and other societal pillars.

Furthermore, the partisan divide in trust levels widened significantly. Republicans and Democrats often exhibited starkly different levels of confidence in the same institutions, reflecting the increasing polarization of American society. For example, trust in the media became highly partisan, with Democrats generally expressing more trust in mainstream news outlets than Republicans. Overall, public opinion data from this period indicated a pervasive sense of national unease and pessimism about the future, reflecting the cumulative impact of major events, a fragmented and often negative media environment, and increasing political and social divisions.

Synthesis and Analysis: Tracing the Interplay Between Media Narratives and National Malaise:

A comparative analysis of media coverage across the decades from the 1960s to the present reveals a notable shift in framing, tone, and focus. Early media narratives, particularly in the initial part of the 1960s, often exhibited a more optimistic and unifying tone, reflecting a greater deference towards authority. However, as the decade progressed and the Vietnam War and Civil Rights Movement gained prominence, media coverage became increasingly critical, exposing societal divisions and questioning government actions. This trend towards a more skeptical and adversarial approach intensified in the 1970s with the Watergate scandal and the economic crisis, where media narratives often highlighted government failures and national vulnerabilities. While the 1980s saw some return to more positive framing with the Reagan era and the end of the Cold War, concerns about social issues and political scandals persisted. The digital age of the 2000s and 2010s has been characterized by highly fragmented and often polarized media narratives, with an increasing focus on conflict, scandal, and negativity across various platforms.

The tendency of news media to emphasize negative events and sensational stories, known as negativity bias, likely plays a significant role in shaping public perception and contributing to a sense of national malaise and decline. Research suggests that negative news tends to have a greater psychological impact on audiences than positive news. In a competitive media environment, the pressure to attract and retain audience attention can incentivize the prioritization of negative and dramatic stories. The 24-hour news cycle and social media platforms, with their constant demand for engagement, may exacerbate this negativity bias by rewarding content that evokes strong emotional responses, often negative ones. This constant exposure to negative narratives, even if reflecting real societal problems, can create a skewed perception of reality, leading to increased cynicism and a belief that things are consistently getting worse.

The evolution of media technologies has fundamentally altered the dissemination and reception of narratives related to national events and societal trends. The rise of television in the 1960s brought unprecedented visual access to events like the Vietnam War and the Civil Rights Movement, profoundly impacting public opinion. The emergence of the Internet and social media in the late 20th and early 21st centuries further revolutionized information sharing, creating a more decentralized and participatory media environment. This shift from a more centralized media landscape, dominated by a few major networks, to a fragmented environment with countless on-line sources and social media platforms has significant implications for the control and framing of narratives. While offering greater access to diverse perspectives, it also presents challenges related to the spread of misinformation, the formation of echo chambers, and the erosion of trust in traditional media sources, potentially contributing to increased cynicism.

Scholarly perspectives on media framing, negativity bias, and public cynicism offer valuable insights into this complex relationship. Media framing theory suggests that the way issues are presented, including the language, imagery, and emphasis used, can significantly influence public opinion and attitudes. Research on negativity bias in media consumption indicates that negative information often has a stronger impact on individuals' perceptions and emotions. The "spiral of cynicism" theory posits that media's focus on political strategy, scandals, and negative framing of political processes can erode public trust in the political system and its actors. These scholarly analyses provide a theoretical framework for understanding how media narratives, particularly those employing negative framing and appealing to negativity bias, can contribute to public cynicism and a sense of national malaise.

Time-line of Major Events, Media Narratives, and Public Opinion Trends (1960s-2010s)

Decade | Key Historical Events | Dominant Media Narratives | Key Public Opinion Trends.

1960s | Civil Rights Movement | Vietnam War escalation | JFK assassination | Counterculture | Exposure of racial inequality | Anti-war sentiment | Shock and uncertainty after assassination | Challenge to mainstream norms | Initial decline in trust in federal government.

1970s | Watergate Scandal | Economic stagflation | End of Vietnam War | Iran Hostage Crisis | Focus on government corruption | Economic hardship and energy crisis | Sense of defeat after Vietnam | National powerlessness | Significant drop in trust in government and other institutions | Sense of national decline.

1980s | Reagan Revolution | End of Cold War | AIDS Epidemic | Iran-Contra Affair | Renewed optimism (initially) Triumph of democracy | Growing concern over social issues | Ethical questions in government | Initial rise in trust for some, but overall trend of cynicism persists.

1990s | End of Cold War | Persian Gulf War | Clinton Impeachment | Rise of Internet | Victory and peace dividend | Lingering concerns over social issues | Ethical lapses in leadership | Early exploration of on-line communication | Continued erosion of trust in government despite economic growth.

2000s | 9/11 Attacks | Wars in Afghanistan and Iraq | Great Recession | National unity then critical war coverage, Economic crisis as systemic failure, Emergence of partisan media | Initial surge in trust then significant decline, Increasing partisan divide in trust.

2010s | Occupy Wall Street, Black Lives Matter, Rise of Social Media, Political Polarization | Focus on inequality and injustice, Amplification of social movements, Spread of misinformation, Deepening partisan divisions | Historically low levels of trust in institutions | Intensified political polarization | Pervasive sense of national unease

Evolution of Media Technologies and their Potential Impact on Narratives of Malaise and Cynicism:

Era	Dominant Media Technologies	Potential Impact on Narrative Dissemination	Potential Impact on Public Perception and Cynicism.
Pre-1960s	Print Media, Radio	Centralized control	slower pace	Shaping national consensus	limited exposure to diverse views.
1960s-1970s	Broadcast Television	Visual impact	broad reach	immediacy	Exposing societal divisions	shifting public opinion (e.g., Vietnam)	fostering distrust in government (Watergate).
1980s-1990s	Cable Television	Early Internet	Increased volume	fragmentation	emergence of partisan outlets	Amplifying negativity	catering to specific viewpoints	early signs of eroding trust in traditional sources
2000s-Present	Internet	Social Media	Decentralized	rapid spread	citizen participation	echo chambers	misinformation	Further fragmentation	amplification of negativity and polarization	erosion of trust in traditional sources	challenges to shared understanding.

Conclusion:

The Enduring Legacy of Media Narratives on American Public Perception and Cynicism.

The analysis presented in this report reveals a consistent and complex interplay between major historical events, media narratives, and the ebb and flow of public opinion and cynicism in the United States from the 1960s to the present day. Media narratives, across news, popular culture, and more recently, social media, have acted as both a reflection of the prevailing national mood and a potential amplifier of feelings of unease and distrust.

Throughout the period examined, significant historical events, from the Civil Rights Movement and the Vietnam War in the 1960s to the Watergate scandal in the 1970s, the economic anxieties of the late 20th and early 21st centuries, and the social and political divisions of the digital age, have provided fertile ground for narratives of national malaise. Media coverage of these events, often characterized by a growing skepticism towards authority and an increasing focus on negative aspects and societal conflicts, has likely contributed to a gradual erosion of public trust in institutions.

The evolution of media technologies has profoundly influenced this dynamic. The advent of television brought the realities of war and social unrest directly into American homes, while the rise of the Internet and social media has created a more fragmented and often polarized information environment. The constant flow of information, coupled with the challenges of misinformation and the formation of echo chambers, has further complicated the relationship between media narratives and public perception, potentially intensifying cynicism.

Finally, the evidence suggests that media narratives have played a significant and multifaceted role in shaping public perception and contributing to the increased cynicism observed in the United States since the 1960s. While media often serves as a crucial source of information and accountability, its inherent negativity bias, the pressures of a competitive and evolving media landscape, and the rise of partisan and social media have created conditions where narratives of national malaise and distrust can readily take hold and potentially amplify existing societal anxieties. Understanding this complex interplay is crucial for navigating the challenges of the contemporary American socio-political landscape and fostering a more informed and engaged citizenry.

Chapter Five:
it was another time…

<u>The "Boomers" and the X Generation:</u>
Those born after WWII and before 1970…are starting to decline in social prominence, and the feeling these Americans are experiencing is a wanton sentiment.

Being great is continually challenged by every new
(improved) American society rank.

These Americans are also endeavoring to clutch as much bravado in personal proficiency and triumphs…which in turn connects to ensuring their lives are of consequence.

The Boomer generation accumulated one métier, the method of how they raised children. This was the final generation to raise whole families at home.

The "Keeping Up with the Jones" kept both parents working in the late 1980s and 90s. Families recognized that to keep their affluent 1980s way of life, both parents ought to work outside the home. This gave way to Boomerang, X-Gen's started moving into the homes of the Boomer Gen to save money or care for aging parents.

The 1980s coerced:
Disillusioned Old Hippies (1960s-era Americans) started to edify other immature American generations: these hippies had the bravado and the credence to create changes for the betterment of American culture.

All the while, they thought that younger Americans were better off because of their dramatic toil and essential perspectives they fought for. This turned hippies into yuppies.

These young urban professional (yuppie) Americans who lived through a crushing defeat in Vietnam equated their generation to be better in every way. Society passed them by in 1970, but now, they are making their voices and thoughts heard. Across the nation, television was evolving to convey the movements' impetus. This was seen with environmental causes, diet, music and most satire trends peaked at this juncture. Luminaries were bred on TV that never could have had America's ear in prior eras. Television divulged illustrations of day-to-day politics and their canards. It was told exceptionally on CBS every night with Walter Cronkite and on NBC's new hit, Not ready for Prime Time Players, later referred to as Saturday Night Live as it became a parody of America's newscast for those willing to stay up to watch. It seemed the shows drew audiences examining the same thing, one in actuality and the other a spin of that reality. Just as prior decades' generation decried the newer generation, these yuppie crowds played down decades of protracted triumphs from other eras because now the genuine civilization was forming. The inception of the "Me Generation" (it is all about Me!) transmitted the exposition of sex, drugs and rock and roll with an extraordinary pace.

Old hipsters that are now being thought of as professionals attempted to acquaint the untried youngsters with what it was like to live during the era where everything you did was to protest and shake up "the man". This is when televisions were filled with reports of upwardly climbing societal evangelists telling you that right is what we say it is. Trying to shape the minds of viewers. A new religion of proper education filled movie houses with what it was like to be part of the greatest generation. Cinema's were filled with past glories and glimpses into a futurist society. It all turned out to be fantasy. One of the known actualities were devalued, so it was easier to consume, and the other obscure enough that it could not be stretched to be actuality. As we look back at those tame visions, it seems reality was scarier.

It was of customary significance to teach the new X-Gen's what it was like to be a relevant social denomination that was able to shape a new American society. It wasn't long before the peaceful protesting gave way to a rowdy anxiety level in America that falsely concocted a new prerequisite for civil controversy and ensured disagreement.

The 1980s saw that colleges changed to a more social teaching of personal rights, to legitimize special social issues, as it shouted out that diversity of life was the key.

Détente of the 1980s set America to surpass the American Malaise.

The American Détente was a strategy of managing ties with a potentially antagonistic country (the USSR) and to preserve harmony while strengthening our vital interests,

Détente was eventually a success because as America's economy strengthened, we could wait out aggressors from the old Soviet Union where their strength dissolved after the end of the Cold War in 1991. It became a wise foreign policy decision for President Ronald Reagan in the long run.

During Reagan's presidency, significant shifts occurred in the federal bureaucracy, driven by his goal to make it more responsive to presidential priorities and less autonomous.

Key Bureaucratic Shifts Under Reagan:

His "Administrative Presidency" Strategy

Reagan adopted and expanded the "administrative presidency," a management approach designed to increase presidential control over the bureaucracy.

This involved appointing large numbers of political loyalists to key positions, especially in Schedule C and non-career Senior Executive Service roles, often using ideological litmus tests to ensure alignment with his agenda.

Strategic appointments allowed Reagan to monitor and direct the activities of career civil servants, bypassing those seen as resistant to his policies.

Centralized Budget and Regulatory Control:
The Office of Management and Budget (OMB) was used aggressively to control agency budgets, dictate funding levels, and enforce cuts, reducing agencies' ability to appeal directly to Congress.

The Office of Information and Regulatory Affairs (OIRA) within OMB was empowered to review and approve all agency regulations, ensuring they matched presidential priorities and limiting independent regulatory action.

Reorganization and Personnel Management:
Reagan's team used reorganization, transfers, and demotions to sideline or remove noncompliant career officials, sometimes employing "hit lists" to target specific individuals. "Jigsaw puzzle management" placed political appointees in line roles traditionally held by career staff, further increasing control and reducing bureaucratic independence.

Mixed Results on Bureaucratic Size:
While Reagan worked with Congress to reduce some aspects of the federal bureaucracy, his expansion of defense and Cold War programs actually increased the number of federal employees in certain areas.

The overall effect was a shift in the bureaucracy's focus and composition, rather than a simple reduction in size.

Long-Term Impact:
These strategies shifted the balance of power from career bureaucrats to presidential appointees, making the bureaucracy more responsive to the White House but also raising

concerns about politicization and the erosion of neutral expertise.

Administrative Presidency Increased use of political appointees, loyalty tests, and direct oversight.

Centralized Budget Control OMB dictated agency budgets, limiting independent agency appeals.

Regulatory Review OIRA reviewed all regulations for alignment with presidential goals.

Personnel Management Transfers, demotions, and reorganization to sideline resistant career staff.

Bureaucratic Size Cuts in some areas, expansion in defense/Cold War programs.

In sum: Reagan's term marked a major shift toward presidential control of the bureaucracy, emphasizing loyalty, centralized oversight, and regulatory restraint, with lasting effects on the structure and culture of federal administration.

Reagan used a comprehensive set of tools—collectively known as the "*administrative presidency*"—to control the federal bureaucracy and ensure it aligned with his policy goals:

Strategic Political Appointments: Reagan dramatically increased the number of political appointees, especially in key management and policy roles. Appointees were often selected based on ideological alignment, using "litmus tests" to ensure loyalty. This allowed the administration to monitor and direct the work of career civil servants and place trusted loyalists in positions of authority.

Centralized Budget Control: The Office of Management and Budget (OMB) was used to dictate agency budgets, set funding levels, and enforce cuts. Agencies were required to submit budgets to OMB, which could then limit their ability to appeal directly to Congress. OMB also managed plans for layoffs and reorganizations, further tightening presidential control.

Regulatory Review: Reagan empowered the OMB's Office of Information and Regulatory Affairs (OIRA) to review and approve all agency regulations. This centralized regulatory review ensured that new rules conformed to presidential priorities and limited independent regulatory action.

Personnel Management and Reorganization: The administration used transfers, demotions, and reorganization to sideline or remove noncompliant career officials. Techniques like "jigsaw puzzle management" placed political appointees in line roles traditionally held by career staff, bypassing resistant bureaucrats and keeping them out of strategic decision-making.

Budget and Personnel Cuts: Reagan implemented budget and personnel cuts to reduce the size and influence of agencies he viewed as obstacles to his agenda.

In summary, Reagan's main tools for controlling the bureaucracy were strategic appointments, centralized budget and regulatory review, aggressive personnel management, and agency reorganization—all designed to make the federal bureaucracy more responsive to presidential direction.

Regenerated Malaise:

The term "malaise" in the context of the U.S. government during the late 1970s and early 1980s is often associated with a sense of disillusionment, economic stagnation, and national insecurity. This period was marked by several interrelated issues that contributed to the public's perception of a crisis in confidence regarding government and American leadership. Here are key aspects of this malaise:

Economic Stagnation:

Stagflation: The U.S. experienced a unique economic phenomenon known as stagflation, characterized by stagnant economic growth, high unemployment, and rising inflation. This was largely driven by the oil crises of the 1970s, which caused energy prices to soar, contributing to economic instability.

High Inflation and Unemployment: By the late 1970s, inflation rates exceeded 10%, while unemployment also rose. Families faced increased costs of living, and many Americans felt squeezed financially. This economic distress contributed to a growing sense of hopelessness.

Energy Crisis:

Oil Embargo: The 1973 oil embargo by OPEC (Organization of Arab Petroleum Exporting Countries) led to widespread fuel shortages and rising prices. A second oil price shock in 1979 further exacerbated the situation, leading to long lines at gas stations and increased inflation.

Energy Policy: The government's response to energy challenges was seen as inadequate. President Jimmy Carter attempted to address the crisis by advocating for conservation and promoting alternative energy sources, but many Americans felt these measures were insufficient.

Political Disillusionment:

Loss of Trust in Government: The Watergate scandal in the early 1970s had already eroded public trust in government and political institutions. By the late 1970s, many Americans felt disillusioned with political leadership, believing that their leaders were unable to solve pressing problems.

Crisis of Confidence Speech: In July 1979, President Carter delivered a speech addressing this malaise, acknowledging the sense of discontent and calling for a national reassessment of priorities. He emphasized the need for unity and a collective effort to overcome challenges, but the speech was seen by many as reflecting a lack of effective solutions.

International Challenges:

Iran Hostage Crisis: In November 1979, the U.S. Embassy in Tehran was stormed, and 52 American diplomats and citizens were taken hostage. The subsequent crisis lasted for 444 days and further diminished public confidence in the government's ability to handle foreign policy and national security.

Soviet Aggression: The Soviet invasion of Afghanistan in December 1979 heightened fears about Soviet expansionism and American vulnerability, compounding feelings of insecurity during this tumultuous period. The Reagan Doctrine became known to fight anticommunist efforts.

Cultural and Social Issues:
Social Change: The late 1970s also witnessed significant social upheaval, including debates over civil rights, women's rights, and sociopolitical movements. These changes, while often positive in the long run, were also met with resistance and conflict, contributing to a sense of instability.
Generational Divide: Younger generations were increasingly questioning authority and traditional values, leading to tensions between different societal factions and contributing to a sense of national discord.

Conclusion:
The malaise of the late 1970s and early 1980s reflects a complex interplay of economic, political, and social factors that contributed to a pervasive sense of disillusionment among many Americans. The sense of crisis in confidence manifested in various ways, including discontent with government, economic fears, and international uncertainty. This atmosphere set the stage for the political changes of the early 1980s, notably the election of Ronald Reagan in 1980, which brought a different approach to governance and economic policy and marked a shift toward a more optimistic outlook among many Americans. The 1980's brought the beginning of a conservative movement in politics.

<u>Trump compared to Reagan's bureaucracy...</u>
Trump's approach to bureaucratic change is highly similar to Reagan's, but even more aggressive in several respects:
Centralization and Political Control: Like Reagan, Trump has sought to increase presidential control over the federal bureaucracy by appointing loyalists to key positions and reclas-

sifying many career civil service roles as political appointees, making it easier to remove or replace them.

Downsizing and Streamlining: Both presidents prioritized shrinking the size of government. Trump implemented hiring freezes, a 10-to-1 deregulation initiative (repealing 10 rules for every new one), and ordered agencies to hire only one new worker for every four who leave.

Targeted Agency Reforms: Trump, like Reagan, used executive orders to reorganize, consolidate, or eliminate agencies and programs he viewed as wasteful or ideologically opposed to his agenda. He established the Department of Government Efficiency to lead these efforts.

Regulatory Rollback: Both administrations aggressively rolled back regulations, but Trump's approach has been even more sweeping, including bypassing traditional public notice and comment processes to speed up deregulation.

Focus on Ideological Alignment: Trump, echoing Reagan, targeted agencies and programs perceived as liberal or resistant, but with a more openly confrontational and punitive tone, especially toward agencies like the EPA and programs related to diversity, equity, and inclusion.

Overall:

Area Reagan (1980s) Trump (2025)

- Political Appointees Increased, loyalty tests Mass reclassification, more direct control
- Downsizing Some cuts, focus on defense Aggressive cuts, hiring freeze, 10-to-1 rule
- Regulatory Policy Deregulation, OMB oversight Sweeping rollback, bypassing procedures
- Targeting Agencies Sidelined resistant staff Fired thousands, targeted "liberal" agencies
- Tone Assertive, strategic More confrontational, punitive

In essence, Trump's bureaucratic changes mirror Reagan's in strategy but are broader in scope and more forceful in execution, aiming for rapid, visible transformation of the federal government.

Empower Your Vision with Reagan Trump: A New Era of Leadership

In a world where influential leaders shape our destiny, it's time to explore the powerful legacies of Ronald Reagan and Donald Trump. Both icons have redefined what it means to lead, inspire, and drive change.

Unlock the wisdom of two great minds:

- Reagan: A beacon of hope and optimism, he championed the values of freedom and prosperity.
- Trump: A bold visionary who challenged the status quo, igniting a movement to put America first.

Each leader brings unique perspectives that empower us to envision a brighter future. Whether you seek strategies for success or inspiration for your journey, learning from their stories can ignite your passion for greatness.

- Dare to dream bigger. Embrace the lessons of Reagan and Trump, and become the leader you were meant to be!

Unite the Legacy: Reagan Meets Trump

In a time when our nation seeks direction and inspiration, the powerful legacies of two iconic leaders, Ronald Reagan and Donald Trump, stand tall. Each has left an indelible mark on America's history, shaping our values and aspirations.

Discover the harmony between tradition and innovation:

Reagan's Vision: A beacon of optimism, championing freedom and opportunity for all.

Trump's Boldness: A testament to resilience, driving change with unapologetic courage.

Together, let their stories inspire a new generation to dream big, embrace challenges, and take action for a brighter tomorrow. Whether you resonate with Reagan's steadfast principles or Trump's dynamic energy, it's time to build on their legacies!

Join us in this journey of inspiration—let's elevate our nation together!

Unite for a Vision: Reagan vs. Trump

In the tapestry of American history, two iconic leaders have shaped our nation's path: Ronald Reagan and Donald Trump. Each brought their unique vision, resilience, and charisma to the forefront of politics, inspiring millions to dream bigger.

- Reagan's hope and optimism: He ignited a spirit of renewal that reminded us of our boundless potential.
- Trump's boldness and tenacity: He challenged the status quo, empowering everyday Americans to reclaim their voice.

This is more than just a comparison; it's an invitation to reflect on the values that define us as a nation. Whether you resonate with Reagan's call for unity or Trump's drive for change, let their legacies inspire you to engage in the conversation about America's future.

Reagan:

Reagan used a comprehensive set of tools—collectively known as the "*administrative presidency*"—to control the federal bureaucracy and ensure it aligned with his policy goals:

Strategic Political Appointments: Reagan dramatically increased the number of political appointees, especially in key management and policy roles. Appointees were often selected based on ideological alignment, using "litmus tests" to ensure loyalty. This allowed the administration to monitor and direct the work of career civil servants and place trusted loyalists in positions of authority.

Centralized Budget Control: The Office of Management and Budget (OMB) was used to dictate agency budgets, set funding levels, and enforce cuts. Agencies were required to submit budgets to OMB, which could then limit their ability to appeal directly to Congress. OMB also managed plans for layoffs and reorganizations, further tightening presidential control.

Regulatory Review: Reagan empowered the OMB's Office of Information and Regulatory Affairs (OIRA) to review and approve all agency regulations. This centralized regulatory review ensured that new rules conformed to presidential priorities and limited independent regulatory action.

Personnel Management and Reorganization: The administration used transfers, demotions, and reorganization to sideline or remove noncompliant career officials. Techniques like "jigsaw puzzle management" placed political appointees in line roles traditionally held by career staff, bypassing resistant bureaucrats and keeping them out of strategic decision-making.

Budget and Personnel Cuts: Reagan implemented budget and personnel cuts to reduce the size and influence of agencies he viewed as obstacles to his agenda.

In summary, Reagan's main tools for controlling the bureaucracy were strategic appointments, centralized budget and regulatory review, aggressive personnel management, and agency reorganization—all designed to make the federal bureaucracy more responsive to presidential direction.

Trump compared to Reagan's bureaucracy...

Trump's approach to bureaucratic change is highly similar to Reagan's, but even more aggressive in several respects:

Centralization and Political Control: Like Reagan, Trump has sought to increase presidential control over the federal bureaucracy by appointing loyalists to key positions and reclassifying many career civil service roles as political appointees, making it easier to remove or replace them.

Downsizing and Streamlining: Both presidents prioritized shrinking the size of government. Trump implemented hiring freezes, a 10-to-1 deregulation initiative (repealing 10 rules for every new one), and ordered agencies to hire only one new worker for every four who leave.

Targeted Agency Reforms: Trump, like Reagan, used executive orders to reorganize, consolidate, or eliminate agencies and programs he viewed as wasteful or ideologically opposed to his agenda. He established the Department of Government Efficiency to lead these efforts.

Regulatory Rollback: Both administrations aggressively rolled back regulations, but Trump's approach has been even more sweeping, including bypassing traditional public notice and comment processes to speed up deregulation.

Focus on Ideological Alignment: Trump, echoing Reagan, targeted agencies and programs perceived as liberal or resistant, but with a more openly confrontational and punitive tone, especially toward agencies like the EPA and programs related to diversity, equity, and inclusion.

Comparison between the two greatest Presidents:
Reagan (1980s) Trump (2025)

- Political Appointees Increased, loyalty tests Mass reclassification, more direct control
- Downsizing Some cuts, focus on defense Aggressive cuts, hiring freeze, 10-to-1 rule
- Regulatory Policy Deregulation, OMB oversight Sweeping rollback, bypassing procedures
- Targeting Agencies Sidelined resistant staff Fired thousands, targeted "liberal" agencies
- Tone Assertive, strategic More confrontational, punitive
- In essence, Trump's bureaucratic changes mirror Reagan's in strategy but are broader in scope and more forceful in execution, aiming for rapid, visible transformation of the federal government.

Empower Your Vision with Reagan Trump: A New Era of Leadership

In a world where influential leaders shape our destiny, it's time to explore the powerful legacies of Ronald Reagan and Donald Trump. Both icons have redefined what it means to lead, inspire, and drive change.

Unlock the wisdom of two great minds:

- Reagan: A beacon of hope and optimism, he championed the values of freedom and prosperity.
- Trump: A bold visionary who challenged the status quo, igniting a movement to put America first.

Each leader brings unique perspectives that empower us to envision a brighter future. Whether you seek strategies for success or inspiration for your journey, learning from their stories can ignite your passion for greatness.

- Dare to dream bigger. Embrace the lessons of Reagan and Trump, and become the leader you were meant to be!

Unite the Legacy: Reagan Meets Trump

In a time when our nation seeks direction and inspiration, the powerful legacies of two iconic leaders, Ronald Reagan and Donald Trump, stand tall. Each has left an indelible mark on America's history, shaping our values and aspirations.

- Discover the harmony between tradition and innovation:
- Reagan's Vision: A beacon of optimism, championing freedom and opportunity for all.
- Trump's Boldness: A testament to resilience, driving change with unapologetic courage.
- Together, let their stories inspire a new generation to dream big, embrace challenges, and take action for a brighter tomorrow. Whether you resonate with Reagan's steadfast principles or Trump's dynamic energy, it's time to build on their legacies!

- Join us in this journey of inspiration—let's elevate our nation together!

Unite for a Vision: Reagan vs. Trump

In the tapestry of American history, two iconic leaders have shaped our nation's path: Ronald Reagan and Donald Trump. Each brought their unique vision, resilience, and charisma to the forefront of politics, inspiring millions to dream bigger.

- Reagan's hope and optimism: He ignited a spirit of renewal that reminded us of our boundless potential.
- Trump's boldness and tenacity: He challenged the status quo, empowering everyday Americans to reclaim their voice.

This is more than just a comparison; it's an invitation to reflect on the values that define us as a nation. Whether you resonate with Reagan's call for unity or Trump's drive for change, let their legacies inspire you to engage in the conversation about America's future.

Reagan and Trump: are both Republican presidents known for promoting conservative values, but their policies, styles, and eras are quite different. Here's a breakdown comparing their major policies and approaches:

Economic Policy:

Ronald Reagan (1981–1989)

- "Reaganomics": Supply-side economics—focused on tax cuts (especially for the wealthy and corporations), deregulation, and reducing government spending (excluding defense).
- Major tax cuts: Economic Recovery Tax Act of 1981.
- Deregulation: Banking, energy, and telecom sectors.
- Huge defense spending increases.
- Result: Economic boom in the mid-80s, but also rising deficits and national debt.

Donald Trump (2017–2021)

- Tax Cuts and Jobs Act (2017): Big corporate tax cut (35% to 21%) and cuts for individuals (tilted toward higher incomes).
- More targeted deregulation: especially environmental rules and financial regulations (e.g., Dodd-Frank rollbacks).
- Trade protectionism: tariffs on China, renegotiated NAFTA → USMCA.
- Economic growth pre-COVID, but deficits also increased.

Foreign Policy::

Reagan:

- Anti-communist: Major focus on fighting the Soviet Union, labeled it "Evil Empire".
- Strong military buildup (Strategic Defense Initiative—"Star Wars").
- Interventions in Latin America (e.g., Nicaragua, Grenada).
- Ended presidency with arms control deals and better relations with Gorbachev.

Trump:

"America First": skeptical of traditional alliances (e.g., NATO), withdrew from international agreements (Paris Climate Accord, Iran nuclear deal).

Cozy with authoritarian leaders (e.g., North Korea's Kim Jong-un, Russia's Putin).

Focused on reducing U.S. involvement abroad (e.g., Afghanistan drawdown).

Immigration:

Reagan:

- More moderate: signed Immigration Reform and Control Act of 1986, which granted amnesty to ~3 million undocumented immigrants but tightened border security and employer sanctions.

Trump:
- Hardline stance: Build the wall, zero tolerance at the border (led to family separations), travel ban from several Muslim-majority countries.
- Drastically reduced legal immigration and refugee intake.

Government and Institutions:

Reagan:
- Advocated limited government, but still worked within traditional political structures.
- Respected institutions like the courts, media, and FBI.

Trump:
- Anti-establishment rhetoric: often attacked the media, FBI, DOJ, and judges.
- Viewed government "deep state" as enemy.
- His presidency ended with the Capitol riot (Jan 6) and refusal to accept 2020 election results, marking a major break from democratic norms.

Political Style:

Reagan:
- "The Great Communicator": optimistic, sunny conservatism.
- Strong believer in American exceptionalism.
- Focused on unity—even when he disagreed with Democrats.

Trump:
- Populist, combative, and divisive.
- Used Twitter to directly attack opponents.
- Focused on loyalty, often turning against former allies.

Reaganomics as a tool that did work:

Reaganomics was an immediate reaction to the malaise's stagflation, industrial decline, and low confidence.

Reagan's upbeat rhetoric, such as his 1981 inaugural address rejecting government as the problem, contrasted with Carter's somber tone, which sought to restore national morale (Reagan Library: Inaugural Address).

By 1983, economic recovery had begun, and the malaise era was widely regarded as over, though debates over whether Reaganomics fully resolved or shifted underlying issues continue.

The Roaring 90s.

It is a time in the home electronic media and computers are being installed in every home which brought additional access to our new society. Our newer generations grew closer together through connectivity of the Internet and older generations of Americans grew further apart and separated faster than in any other decade because of the lack of connectivity. Commonly segregated society norms of the big cities popular culture spread and intermixed instantaneously across an entire nation without physical distance barriers slowing them.

"Pop Culture" was in full bloom in the 1990s. It was the time of excess and peace in the overt world. The culture was seen, and we interacted with the advent of nationwide hit shows that produced valuable commodities like toys that had animated personalities broadcast on TV and, kids shows that spawned blessed young adult stars that never knew hardship. Grunge rock was born and adopted easily by America's rebellious youth. Americans super sized their food options and their media consumption. Disney cartoon classics paved the way for multi million dollar budget movies that didn't need real people on a stage providing the entertainment. Google made everyone's life better, becoming an easy-to-use encyclopedia.

The collapse of the Soviet Union had less importance to us as a Nation than did MTV. MTV, for its purpose, becomes a mass indoctrination of newly allowed societal norms where anything can be accepted and should be exalted. From hairstyles, to music, to religion could be the new cool trend for the entire population of American youth.

There is no more separation of American rural stance and big city mindset. They mix and are accepted instantaneously. The global economy started in its infancy as it bore the European Union. A force that might slow communism across Europe. Germany reunited after nearly fifty years.

A daunting spectacle that many Presidents presided over yet could not change. With the joining of Germany's East and West, it became the superpower economy in Europe. Years of heartache were soon forgotten, and Europe grew more politically powerful.

Weather became a national tragedy, with hurricane Andrew landing near Miami to cause 25 billion in damage. It was the worst natural disaster in America's history at that time. Time passes and the regularity of powerful storms has changed. There have been many cat, 5 storms since, but Andrew was a wake-up call to change our environment. Decades have passed, but many people in Florida still measured how their lives were affected by Hurricane Andrew.

The sands of the Middle East were bloodied, but not with American lives. This was a time of computerized strikes and aerial assaults that won a war without an uncivilized amount of American deaths. It was also a time when hostilities in Ireland calmed to the point when you spoke about the meaning of IRA, you were talking about your finances. Cloning started and another phase in human history that until now was a moral challenge, not a technical one.

The nineties also produced an elite terrorist culture. The first World Trading Center bomb exploded, killing less than 10 but injuring over one thousand Americans. What was next to be seen would unquestionably be hell on earth.

President Clinton signed into law "don't ask, don't tell" for military servicemen. An American Malaise, once again caused by the government, yet many people didn't think it was necessary in the first place. Years later it was re-walked by President Obama and canceled.

This of course has led us to today, with one of our military officers running around military bases in a dress.

Ex-football great OJ Simpson gets away with murder on TV. His televised case was must-see TV for all 95 million watching Americans. He was later tried by the parents of Ron Goldstein, and he was found guilty of their deaths and fined 33.5 million dollars. Of course, he never paid the court's decision, he left for Florida because you can not have your assets and property taken from a liable court decision. Later, he commits armed robbery and kidnapping, which finally ends up with him in jail. His story has spun multiple TV documentaries and spoofs. Songs and video games have featured his dubious acts within them.

President Clinton is investigated, tried and found guilty of lying to the American public. A 49-year-old lawyer and President of the United States perjured himself because he didn't think there was a problem having an affair with a 22-year-old woman in the Oval office. Later, the President ended up in contempt of the court case by giving misleading testimony during these trials. And all of this was after the Whitewater scandal years before. This was all on display for Americans getting ready to vote between Al Gore and George Bush (43). Clinton's fatigue and its onslaught malaise plagued the democrats until Obama.

Nearing 2000 (Y2k):

The turn of the century saw the first generation in America that grew up owning multiple computing Technologies.

The very end of 1999 saw the Dow Jones Industrials rise above 10,000 level. This was driven by the way our government functioned. People voted for the next administration with their pocket books. Times were good and everyone seemed to be living the "American Dream". All the while, we are preparing for the Y2K bug that never happened. Computers drive all industry and human life in America. Without computers running the systems that rely upon them, American life would not be the same. The Chinese government saw this episode as a striking point against America and started with their plans on taking back Taiwan, which has become the major producer of computer chips over these decades.

Each of these occurrences brings a new activation, dimension, and speed to actual social engagement. The Media rises from cable's superiority in connectivity. We are as dependent on the Internet as we were on TV in the 60s and 70s. Gen X sets a pace for the cross-cultural mixing of families. It is a cross-cultural country. Our society is no longer mostly of white European ancestors. Our values as a nation are changing quickly. Differences in the way you should live life are thought out and are driven by someone else's opinion. This is seen stretching across America faster than ever before via home computers and newer smart phones. The advent of smart devices blooms into a world changing media platform. These platforms are used to drive what someone else appraises as important in this new, ever-changing American society. After 50 years of pride in "being who you are," it is now seen as hatred. You be you, and I'll be me is commonly the reply to statements about how you live your life.

<u>The Fall of the Towers on 911...</u>
Brought us together as an American family in 2001
as much as the race to the Moon did in the 1960s.

2001 saw the Presidency of the US tested like it was in the 1960s. The comparative worldwide implications were felt in every country around the world. It took many years to find and destroy a menace of terrorists, yet America stayed on track to finish the job. The missing towers were a daily reminder of the commitment fellow Americans have to one another. After the malaise that followed with multiple years of battling, America didn't show signs of diminishing. Disillusionment was no longer ours.

After the Towers fell in New York, we saw American pride on display in every American neighborhood. It was a statement from all of us. "America is still here, you could not diminish our pride in America and we are on our way back." Being able to say we were one of those Americans gives goosebumps even today. No matter where you lived, what part of America or its friendly nations across the world, these terrible events ultimately brought people together, which produced a global pride in the recovery and America's nationhood strength.

It was not angst against the people that committed these acts, or the nations that birthed this terrorist, it was the oneness of being American that turned our distrust of one party or another to a point where all Americans were side by side to find and defeat anyone that would sneak attack America.

<u>World events and a new start?</u>
What is America going to repeat?
Taiwan is the key to America staying a relevant
superpower and economic leader.

War is on the horizon with the Chinese Communist Party… and America's disillusionment will be complete if America fails this test. It seems as though we are doomed to failure and strife again. Only to be brought down by a developing 150-year plan of the communists to rule the world.

There is a historical precedent for this idea. In Operation Paperclip, immediately after World War II, the United States and its allies evacuated more than 1,500 scientists and engineers from Germany. The American technological edge so crucial to the military balance in the Cold War would have been more tenuous, too.

The free world may soon face the same dilemma it had in 1945. The United States and its Communist rivals are racing to take the technological edge in an emerging Cold War. Taiwan's semiconductor engineers would play a comparable role as German scientists in a contemporary Space Race to construct an advanced and secure chip supply chain. The success of Operation Paperclip for Taiwan could be the decisive factor for the democratic world's victory over its authoritarian adversaries.

… It would also hit at the heart of the American economy. It is time for us to look to the beginning of the last Cold War for ways to ensure that even if deterrence fails, the American economy won't. Losing Taiwan to the communist Chinese would represent more than the tragic death of Taiwanese democracy and a military disaster for the United States.

Chapter Six:

What has this disillusionment begot?
An entire population is working against half of
itself every election cycle.

How Bureaucracy Breeds Government Inefficiency
Layers and Rules Create Structural Barriers

Government bureaucracy is inherently prone to inefficiency due to its monopolistic nature, lack of competition, and entrenched systems. Unlike private businesses that must adapt to consumer demands and face market pressures, government agencies operate in protected environments, leading to wasteful practices and poor service delivery.

Bureaucratic inertia—resistance to change and slow decision-making—arises as agencies accumulate layers of administration, oversight, and regulation. This complexity hinders flexibility, slows innovation, and makes it difficult to respond quickly to new challenges.

Rules and procedures, often created to ensure accountability or prevent abuse, can become so cumbersome that they paralyze effective action. Initiating new projects or policies requires navigating a maze of approvals and regulations, resulting in delays and resource waste.

Lack of Accountability and Incentives:

Government employees typically enjoy greater job security and are less directly accountable to performance outcomes compared to private-sector workers. This reduces incentives to innovate, cut waste, or improve service quality.

Budgeting often focuses on securing future funding or maintaining bureaucratic structures rather than delivering results, leading to resource mis allocation and redundant efforts.

Regulatory Capture and Mission Creep:

Regulatory agencies can fall victim to "regulatory capture," where they serve the interests of the industries they regulate rather than the public, resulting in policies that perpetuate inefficiency and benefit only powerful players.

Agencies may expand their mandates beyond their original purposes ("mission creep"), creating bloated structures that dilute effectiveness and further increase inefficiency.

Private vs. Government Bureaucracy:

- Aspect-Private Sector | Government Bureaucracy
- Competition- High (drives efficiency) | Low/None (breeds inefficiency)
- Accountability-Direct (to customers/shareholders) Indirect (to taxpayers/voters)
- Incentives-Profit, innovation, survival Job security, budget preservation
- Flexibility-High (can adapt quickly) Low (slow, rigid processes)
- Response to Failure-Rapid correction or exit Persistent inefficiency

America's government has grown increasingly complex and top-heavy, with a vast bureaucracy now responsible for implementing an ever-expanding array of policies and regulations. This growth has led to inefficiency, waste, and a system that struggles to deliver on its promises.

Key Factors Behind Bureaucratic Overload:
- The federal government employs millions across 438 departments, agencies, and sub-agencies, with most positions insulated from electoral changes and accountability.

- The number and complexity of public policies have multiplied over recent decades, but administrative resources have not kept pace, resulting in agencies being under-resourced relative to their responsibilities.
- Overlapping programs and duplicative efforts waste billions annually, as highlighted by repeated calls to cut unnecessary entities and advisory committees.
- Structural factors—like the bicameral legislative system, checks and balances, and poor coordination between agencies—further slow decision-making and service delivery.
- Bureaucratic inertia and union protections make it difficult to remove ineffective employees, compounding inefficiency.
- Judicial deference to agency expertise (such as the Chevron doctrine) has allowed bureaucrats to expand their authority beyond what the Founders intended, reducing direct accountability to voters.

In the 1970s, several factors contributed to the growing power and influence of bureaucracies in the United States. Here are some of the key reasons and contexts that led to this trend:

Expansion of Government Responsibilities:
Social Programs: The 1960s Great Society programs initiated by President Lyndon B. Johnson expanded the role of the federal government in areas such as healthcare, education, and poverty reduction. These initiatives required the establishment and growth of bureaucratic agencies to implement and manage these programs effectively.

Environmental Regulation: Rising concerns about environmental issues, epitomized by events like the first Earth Day in 1970, led to the establishment of regulatory agencies such as the Environmental Protection Agency (EPA). The creation of these agencies increased the scope and power of bureaucracies as they developed regulations and enforcement mechanisms.

Economic Challenges:

Stagflation and Energy Crisis: The economic problems of the 1970s, including stagflation (high inflation combined with stagnant economic growth) and the oil crisis, prompted government interventions in the economy. Bureaucracies played critical roles in managing economic policies, regulating industries, and responding to crises.

Deregulation Movements: As a counterpoint, there were also movements toward deregulation in some sectors toward the end of the decade, particularly in transportation and communications. In such cases, bureaucracies had to adapt to new regulatory frameworks while also grappling with their existing mandates.

Increased Public Expectations:

Citizen Participation: The 1960s and 1970s saw a rise in activism, with citizens demanding more accountability and services from their government. This public engagement created a context in which agencies were expected to take on more responsibility in terms of service delivery and regulation.

Consumer Protection: Growing consumer advocacy movements led to the establishment of agencies and regulations focused on protecting consumer rights, further increasing the influence and power of bureaucracies in daily life.

Legislation Leading to Bureaucratic Growth:

Key Legislation: Significant legislation in the 1970s, such as the Occupational Safety and Health Act (OSHA) and various civil rights laws, required robust bureaucratic structures to enforce compliance and protect citizens' rights.

Health and Safety Regulations: As concerns about workplace safety, product safety, and public health rose, the need for bureaucratic agencies with specialized knowledge and authority to create and enforce regulations grew.

Crisis Management:

Response to National Crises: The 1970s included several national crises, including the aftermath of the Vietnam War, the Watergate scandal, and economic challenges. During these crises, bureaucracies often became central to government responses, leading to a perception of their power and importance in promoting national stability.

Judicial Support:

Judicial Activism: The courts in the 1970s sometimes supported the expansion of bureaucratic authority, affirming the need for agencies to have the power to create rules and regulations. This judicial endorsement provided bureaucracies with a stronger legal standing in their operations.

Overall, the 1970s were a period of significant growth and empowerment for bureaucracies in the United States due to the combination of expanding governmental responsibilities, public expectations for service and accountability, and legislative mandates.

These factors established a more prominent role for bureaucratic institutions in the governance and administration of the country, a trend that has continued in various forms into subsequent decades.

Programs often fail to meet public needs due to poor implementation and lack of resources.

The administrative state's growth has diluted the influence of elected officials and the public, undermining representative democracy.

Efforts to reform and streamline government—such as executive orders to eliminate waste and reduce unnecessary agencies—aim to restore efficiency and accountability, but face institutional resistance.

Bureaucratic overload has made the U.S. government less responsive, less efficient, and less accountable, with a sprawling administrative state that often fails to deliver on its promises to the American people.

Government bureaucracy's layers, rigid rules, and lack of competition foster systemic inefficiency. Attempts to reform often miss these deeper structural issues, while inefficiency persists due to bureaucratic inertia, lack of accountability, regulatory capture, and mission creep.

Shifts happening now:
During Reagan's presidency, significant shifts occurred in the federal bureaucracy, driven by his goal to make it more responsive to presidential priorities and less autonomous.

Key Bureaucratic Shifts Under Reagan
The "Administrative Presidency" Strategy:
Reagan adopted and expanded the "administrative presidency," a management approach designed to increase presidential control over the bureaucracy.

This involved appointing large numbers of political loyalists to key positions, especially in Schedule C and noncareer Senior Executive Service roles, often using ideological litmus tests to ensure alignment with his agenda.

Strategic appointments allowed Reagan to monitor and direct the activities of career civil servants, bypassing those seen as resistant to his policies.

Centralized Budget and Regulatory Control:
The Office of Management and Budget (OMB) was used aggressively to control agency budgets, dictate funding levels, and enforce cuts, reducing agencies' ability to appeal directly to Congress.

The Office of Information and Regulatory Affairs (OIRA) within OMB was empowered to review and approve all agency regulations, ensuring they matched presidential priorities and limiting independent regulatory action.

Reorganization and Personnel Management:
Reagan's team used reorganization, transfers, and demotions to sideline or remove noncompliant career officials, sometimes employing "hit lists" to target specific individuals.

"Jigsaw puzzle management" placed political appointees in line roles traditionally held by career staff, further increasing control and reducing bureaucratic independence.

Mixed Results on Bureaucratic Size:
While Reagan worked with Congress to reduce some aspects of the federal bureaucracy, his expansion of defense and Cold War programs actually increased the number of federal employees in certain areas.

The overall effect was a shift in the bureaucracy's focus and composition, rather than a simple reduction in size.

Long-Term Impact:
These strategies shifted the balance of power from career bureaucrats to presidential appointees, making the bureaucracy more responsive to the White House but also raising concerns about politicization and the erosion of neutral expertise.

In sum:
- Administrative Presidency; Increased use of political appointees, loyalty tests, and direct oversight
- Centralized Budget Control; OMB dictated agency budgets, limiting independent agency appeals
- Regulatory Review; OIRA reviewed all regulations for alignment with presidential goals

- Personnel Management; Transfers, demotions, and reorganization to sideline resistant career staff
- Bureaucratic Size Cuts in some areas, expansion in defense/Cold War programs

In sum, Reagan's term marked a major shift toward presidential control of the bureaucracy, emphasizing loyalty, centralized oversight, and regulatory restraint, with lasting effects on the structure and culture of federal administration.

Reagan used a comprehensive set of tools—collectively known as the "*administrative presidency*"—to control the federal bureaucracy and ensure it aligned with his policy goals:

Strategic Political Appointments: Reagan dramatically increased the number of political appointees, especially in key management and policy roles. Appointees were often selected based on ideological alignment, using "litmus tests" to ensure loyalty. This allowed the administration to monitor and direct the work of career civil servants and place trusted loyalists in positions of authority.

Centralized Budget Control: The Office of Management and Budget (OMB) was used to dictate agency budgets, set funding levels, and enforce cuts. Agencies were required to submit budgets to OMB, which could then limit their ability to appeal directly to Congress. OMB also managed plans for layoffs and reorganizations, further tightening presidential control.

Regulatory Review: Reagan empowered the OMB's Office of Information and Regulatory Affairs (OIRA) to review and approve all agency regulations. This centralized regulatory review ensured that new rules conformed to presidential priorities and limited independent regulatory action.

Personnel Management and Reorganization: The administration used transfers, demotions, and reorganization to sideline or remove noncompliant career officials. Techniques like "jigsaw puzzle management" placed political appointees in line roles traditionally held by career staff, bypassing resistant bureaucrats and keeping them out of strategic decision-making.

Budget and Personnel Cuts: Reagan implemented budget and personnel cuts to reduce the size and influence of agencies he viewed as obstacles to his agenda.

Reagan's main tools for controlling the bureaucracy were strategic appointments, centralized budget and regulatory review, aggressive personnel management, and agency reorganization—all designed to make the federal bureaucracy more responsive to presidential direction.

<u>Obama's inclination:</u>

When people talk about Obama-era policies increasing bureaucracies, they're generally referring to the expansion of federal agencies or regulations during his presidency. Here's a breakdown of the main areas where that perception comes from:

Affordable Care Act (ACA or "Obamacare")

Expansion of oversight: The ACA created new bodies like the Center for Medicare and Medicaid Innovation and expanded the role of Health and Human Services (HHS).

State-level exchanges: Though administered locally, they had to comply with federal standards, adding complexity and coordination layers.

Dodd-Frank Wall Street Reform Act

New agencies created: Most notably, the Consumer Financial Protection Bureau (CFPB) was created to regulate financial products and protect consumers.

Expanded roles: Agencies like the Securities and Exchange Commission (SEC) and Federal Reserve received new powers and responsibilities.

Environmental Policies:

EPA empowerment: The Environmental Protection Agency (EPA) took a more active role under Obama, especially with regulations on carbon emissions (like the Clean Power Plan).

Critics argued this increased red tape for industries like energy, agriculture, and manufacturing.

Education Initiatives:

Race to the Top and Common Core incentives: Though not direct federal mandates, they encouraged states to adopt reforms in exchange for federal funds, often requiring new state-level administrative structures.

General Increase in Regulation:

Between 2009 and 2016, thousands of new federal rules were issued, some requiring new offices or expanded roles within existing agencies to enforce and monitor compliance.

Supporters' View:

Many of these expansions were seen as necessary to modernize, protect public welfare, and prevent future crises (especially post-2008 financial crash and health care challenges).

Critics' View:

Critics argue that these policies ballooned federal bureaucracy, increased government overreach, and slowed economic growth due to increased regulation.

Trump compared to Reagan's bureaucracy...

Trump's approach to bureaucratic change is highly similar to Reagan's, but even more aggressive in several respects:

Centralization and Political Control: Like Reagan, Trump has sought to increase presidential control over the federal bureaucracy by appointing loyalists to key positions and reclassifying many career civil service roles as political appointees, making it easier to remove or replace them.

Downsizing and Streamlining: Both presidents prioritized shrinking the size of government. Trump implemented hiring freezes, a 10-to-1 deregulation initiative (repealing 10 rules for every new one), and ordered agencies to hire only one new worker for every four who leave.

Targeted Agency Reforms: Trump, like Reagan, used executive orders to reorganize, consolidate, or eliminate agencies and programs he viewed as wasteful or ideologically opposed to his agenda. He established the Department of Government Efficiency to lead these efforts.

Regulatory Rollback: Both administrations aggressively rolled back regulations, but Trump's approach has been even more sweeping, including bypassing traditional public notice and comment processes to speed up deregulation.

Focus on Ideological Alignment: Trump, echoing Reagan, targeted agencies and programs perceived as liberal or resistant, but with a more openly confrontational and punitive tone, especially toward agencies like the EPA and programs related to diversity, equity, and inclusion.

In sum:

Reagan (1980s)   /   Trump (2025)

- Political Appointees Increased, loyalty tests Mass reclassification, more direct control
- Downsizing Some cuts, focus on defense Aggressive cuts, hiring freeze, 10-to-1 rule
- Regulatory Policy Deregulation, OMB oversight Sweeping rollback, bypassing procedures
- Targeting Agencies Sidelined resistant staff Fired thousands, targeted "liberal" agencies
- Tone Assertive, strategic. More confrontational, punitive

In essence, Trump's bureaucratic changes mirror Reagan's in strategy but are broader in scope and more forceful in execution, aiming for rapid, visible transformation of the federal government.

People submitting to the ideal of unity are found to be the worst therapists to others looking for a commitment of unification.

In our political nature, we have to take sides. Now, since no one political party trusts the other, their citizenry follows. Thinking about it, it is the extremes in each party that the other party recognizes more frequently, and it is how they are evaluated. Like, not all democrats think we should abort babies up until the moment they are born.

The political disengaged are even more illiterate to the differences in the political structure of our citizens. Other people's political evaluations of one side or another is driven by what they see and read in the media. If you only watch MSNBC, you would only know that Hillary Clinton had her presidential election stolen from her, not that our system uses an electoral college to elect candidates. Where the college has boundaries and rules to electing officials. It is not the actual vote numbers in total, it is decided by how many votes from Senators and Representatives, delineating differing and separate parts of the U.S. vote.

It seems that we like to take sides. Sometimes it is a family tradition, like the Kennedy's. Until now. Robert Jr.'s split from the Democrats, an audible grown could be heard across the world from disillusioned Kennedy family followers. As he stated, he pursued ingrained "old democrat" beliefs running now as an independent, he feels more in-line with their policy than the current Democratic Party. Many believe he is going to have to tell people you can ride the fence of politics. He will have to make his case why he left the party. Having heard this from older democrats, "the political party has left me". Americans assume many others in the old party might follow him because he is representing their previously held values and beliefs.

He will have to inform his old party why they should feel good about their move to the mutual ideals with a different party name. He'll need to be humble about his jumping parties and tell everyone, anyone, can feel good about this change. Be positive about the ultimate change. It is a change made from following his conviction and conscience, not the family history. There will surely be many drawn to his station and posture with his usual Kennedy charm and wit.

He will need to encourage his followers to believe their need to be legitimate in their convictions instead of evenly apportioning consent in unification. He will need to evolve the differences into constructive commonalities. To do this, he will have to call out his old political bosses. He must downplay the new independent political zealots at the fringe of the party.

Bernie is always calling for socialization of the political party it should help Kennedy differentiate himself from the newer parts of his old party.

Kennedy will need help telling current democrats why an Independent Democratic should now represent them, building upon practical social trusts. It will be a larger table to set. He will have to walk the line on both viewpoints and global theory of each of their parties' political customs. It might be the start of a new tradition for families across America.

Governmental standardized teaching facilities offer education in seemingly unproductive courses...

The governing regulations within this convocation also and most always contradict previously held norms and values. Why shouldn't colleges provide courses that use histories and memoirs of mankind's achievements to show a new mind that way to the future. No, instead, colleges have courses helping to distract minds from important issues and ethics. 40% of college grads say they were not equipped to go into the workforce after college. They complain about not having socialization skills and language skills for business. Businessmen say the college grads have little experience in the type of work they need to do after classes end. It sounds like a hands-on Vo-tech style of learning has to be included into college curriculum.

Why would any student that wasn't going into teaching take courses like history of racist democrats, or trans-phobic might be an essential job criterion.

Our youth has lost valued ethics for decades, seduced into obtaining these counterproductive and diminished education standards as achievable goals to a degree, and then use them in career prosperity. A surely better way is to tell all learn-ate abstruse understudies, before you go and spend your mom and dad's money, "why are you going to college?" To learn a skill to use for getting a business related job. Have you ever asked potential career field employers what they're looking for in a degree employee? Most times it is the ability to do something, not what you know about gender studies.

Their educators are only partially reckless. The entire highly compensated instructional and guidance dominion is at fault. To fulfill their need for self-gratitudes and highly lauded applause, they overstate the importance of their teachings for real world job requirements. A partially guilty society is to blame for requiring some classes that you will never need outside higher learning. Has anyone ever wondered why they had to learn algebra? Americans hardly ever used it in the rest of their lives outside of school. Because the frivolousness of rewards amassed, re-instruction at the company level is needed as one enters a chosen field of endeavor. Entire decades of our citizenry have been disillusioned in the value of these useless accreditations.

The ideals of self-sufficiency are replaced with aspiration of complacency in victim-hood...

Developing life filled with personal gains are abandoned, replaced, and immersed into someone's "wronged me" disposition. The way to get through this is to ask yourself, what do I think about these occurrences? If it seems more and more to you that things going on around you are directed at you to hurt you in some way, you have become the issue. Your victim-hood is plain to see. Stop thinking that you will always be a victim of someone else's impulses.

Think outside of feeling that you don't have any control of what happens to you. You do! You just have to do it, as the saying goes.

Complacency is the worst type of "oh I can't change anything". Or, owning it to play into someone's sympathies. As they are easier on you, you learn to be even more of a victim to get things handed to you. Being morally ethical can also be an advantage in victim-hood. Being a morally ethical person can make others worship or dislike you. The one example of this is the WWII soldier who wouldn't fight in battle but ended up saving 50 of his fellow soldiers in the war.

This ultimately stunts your ability to see the world as it is today. In some cases, you can not see the plight of others because the need to be a victim is too strong for you to overlook. Being able to see past this, you will recognize others are victims. You feel that your hardships are more than other people's struggles. This will give you a two-sided feeling of reality, and you will always take your side over others. You need to stop it!

Angst and disenchantment in fellow elected political party members...

Political parties are so distant from the norms of our culture from just a previous generation.

The organized special interest groups have found commonality in partitioning our citizenry as it claims to gather a lagging country. As they divide, they can claim more power from doing so. Dividing Americans along race and social sect is seen too commonly. An astute politician recognizes this and speaks to it. Requiring other civil servants to admit to using them and then declare why it is occurring and that it must be wrong for public servants to use these mandates.

In the political classes, the runner-up from the previous loss in an election builds his infrastructure more quickly than the first time around. They have a built-in "you are next up" in this field because you have worked into the system. Your donor base recognizes your name out of a crowd of 4 to a dozen candidates in most instances. The colleagues that might be elected currently will help the next class because they will have seniority over the subsequent notable in the line. Seniority breeds conceit as quickly as ultimate power. It is the power that colleagues place in a re-elected official that becomes too prized and paralyzing to let go. This appetite for esteem and influence only gets aggrandized after it has led to many re-elections. In reality, a permanent elected class, not the people, has ultimate power in this decade. The decades turn into new yet stagnant government bureaucracies without end. An FBI and CIA without a leash. Spying on US citizens and working against an entire populace is seen and not commented upon.

It takes less than one generation to lose previously held common convictions. President Reagan made his most famous speeches about how we should not lean on our government. The government should not be allowed to help in most cases. It causes uncertainty and curtains development then expands leverage for the bureaucracy.

The worst of empowerment is noticed in governmental bodies. Ultimately, power corrupts. The US is seeing an unregulated governance doing whatever it pleases. A citizenry has forfeited its self-determination as it allocates more of its autonomy in exchange for assistance from these bureaucracies.

<u>As of Late:</u>
Rather than the 'polite and orderly stewards of America's deterioration' that Florida Senator Marco Rubio had anticipated, Biden and his minions are neither polite nor orderly and have allowed a precipitous, chaotic, and possibly irreversible decay of a nation whose contributions to planetary culture are arduous to exaggerate. Who can ignore the infamy of the fall of Kabul, Afghanistan, in August 2021, a debacle that resulted in the loss of hundreds of innocent lives, including 13 American warriors blown to pieces by an Islamic State suicide bomber as they readied to vacate? And the state-of-the-art weaponry valued at more than $85 billion dollars was left behind by the retreating Americans, much of which fell into the hands of terrorists who wish to do damage to the United States and her allies?

Nothing says you are a declining superpower and have lost your willingness to retain your position on the multinational stage more than what occurred in Kabul. No wonder Putin felt empowered to attack Ukraine six months later; and Chinese emissaries, representing a nation that incarcerates disfavored minorities in concentration camps and forcibly harvests the organs of detainees and other marginalized people for profit, felt entirely at ease lecturing their US peers on human liberties and how inadequately America treats its citizens of African lineage.

A world of mistrust in once world-wide friends and societies. Once thought of as a country that could not get out of its own way is now seemingly the home of separation abilities in unleashing "Covid." The Chinese government still denies the truth yet might be said to be sorrowful. Their mistrust in their own citizenry should tell us the real story. When the British gave up the rights to Hong Kong and the Chinese told the world nothing will change, all of it did.

The citizens of Hong Kong regularly asked President Trump to come in and rescue them from the totalitarian Chinese government. Once the Chinese set their sites on a target, it is just a matter of time. No matter the reassurance they state, the Chinese will acquire what they want and change provinces and countries forever. Let's just remember, they have always said the Chinese will always plan on reunifying the two Chinese governments. Taiwan has to be the next nation they acquire. This will destroy the world as we know it now, because 80 % or more of the world's supply of semiconductors are manufactured on the island nation. The Chinese with one move can control most modern, important computer-based societies. This could be the ultimate pandemic.

This brings a suggestion for a worldwide scramble to counterbalance this menace to begin. As people fight just to stay free of Chinese control, statewide and countrywide governmental takeovers to protect their societies will ensue. Governments' preparative actions are going to lock physical and intellectual borders. It will cause other governments to take advantage of the lack of rules or create drastic rules to keep themselves in power. Look at Cambodia after Vietnam fell. A Genocide occurred that killed as many as three million. The government of the Khmer Rouge brought citizens out of Phhon Penn (the Capital) and into forced labor. They killed one in four citizens from starvation or execution. Rules of modern society will change in many parts of the world.

Lock-downs and other formalities will take advantage of disparate times. Decorum and rules will lax, and governments will test to see what they can push onto their citizenry.

Societies will push back on their governments as the elected officials try to speed into a new look for their governments. A worldwide paralyzing plague of governmental control will become uniform across worldwide communities. Individual countries will have to fight one another to stay essentially viable, while their lawmakers demand exceedingly harsh and inescapable compulsions for the citizens that they should care about. There can be only one time when we can go through another world's great reset. Societies today are too fragile and will break down into tribalism quickly.

Ties crumble, and spreading tribalism becomes the
norm across America. A tribal world is the regretful
result across the world.
This makes us less strong.

Tribalism through history was to protect groups of common peoples. Sometimes having one chieftain to represent all other members in that society. They did it for common protection from others that didn't have the same common morals, desires and needs. It was used to form the beginning of government. And today, governments are formed to protect its people. When a society is formed under the protection of the government, it will stand together longer than separated by uncommon traits. The way a specific language holds together a country or region or, even, becomes the boundaries of a continent like South America. The Brazilians only speak Portuguese. It isn't spoken elsewhere in the world unless there is a Portuguese governing body. Spanish (in some form or dialect) brings the rest of the continent together with language.

An America that isn't strong of will and
in its economy, it will fail.

Lincoln knew this well. He told us
"A house divided can not stand"...

It could not have been stated better. America has to be against Tribalism, so the world does not fall apart. Any agency or government that heralds this Tribalism is looking to start its own dismantling and demise. These agencies are only looking to lessen the commonality of a country's peoples, so it boosts their own power in the sparest people they represent. Hitler knew this worked well. To bring his country out of economic decline, he created a war machine that built a nation on the falsehood about the Jewish people. He united his select groups of common peoples under his leadership. His plan was to unite all Germanic peoples, and WWII was formulated and methodism.

These new agencies boasting a tribal climate around the world are using that theory in the same manner to keep us from gathering resistance to their formula. The idea of separate and conquer is the perfect strategy in modern political life. It is seen more and more in daily speeches and political rallies. Keeping the world's population tribal does this. It lets others create a false sense where it could be used to separate from others and have only like-minded peoples in Utopian villages. Global initiatives used to raise one small group of people over another is what our government is giving us now. By blistering a single group of America over and past another group creates this internal national Tribalism. Just as the Southern States said they were more alike than the entire scope of the United States, it fed the southern state separatist ways in the 1840s and 50s. The end of the Civil War brought America back from a disastrous tribalism Malaise.

The only thing tying the commonality of the population is the fact that they might have trusted a governmental agency to help. President Reagan famously told Americans the government was the stumbling block for our economic freedoms. He led the way for future limiting governmental interference

196

in Americans' lives. He fixed the poor economy he inherited from President Carter by cutting the regulations that were holding back invention and progress. His stance was to get out of the way and let the experts lead us out of a downward fiscal cascade. Capitalism was unleashed with a build up in the military that created jobs to provide necessities to the armed forces. The up-tick in the military was not limited to overt tactics, but covert military operations thrived, given the leaders in South America hesitation to be the cause of controversy in our part of the world.

In a way, Reagan brought the right help from the government to people desiring it the most….freedom loving countries trying to block socialism in our hemisphere.

The captains of industry, once paralyzed by political based regulations, were freed to do what they do best. Grow and bring along the middle class for the rise upward. Bureaucracy and their sibling agencies only look to expand their grasp in your life. Reagan showed us that in the 90s.

Whenever they help you, families lose a once granted freedom or self dignity, and they become intertwined and seemingly dissoluble aspects in your way of life. It is like they grow more powerful by how much they can get you to leech off the system, becoming totally dependent on their support. That support is all encompassing, and you become intertwined so much that one can't survive with the other fulfilling your needs and their need for more control over your life. They need your support so they can keep their power, you need them willing to give you support, so you can supposable make your way in our society.

This is how America failed the Civil Rights movement. Looking past the achievements that were gained in public segregation, the Black citizens of America were always pawns of the system and never reached a level of king or queen on the American chess board. The government created a life and lifestyle where once you get attached to the benefits, you never want to give them back.

The disillusionment of entire generations of Black Americans have endured and was accelerated to this day because the government thought what they offered helped. It literally captured an entire populace of Americans, trapping them in a spinning hamster wheel.

All of this has brought little change in the help given to Black Americans. Before the 60s, black poverty rate was 32% in America. Today it is still 21% after decades of help from the government. Some offer up the fact that in the 1960s, Black families had two adults in the home raising their kids. Today 70% of Black households have one parent and mostly the mother only is caring for the family. Poverty and females at the head of the household have become familiar and unduly commonplace. What was positively felt across Black America were the graduation rates are much higher today than in yesteryear.

Because of disillusionment at home, world leaders have no reasons to trust the US any more than does our own Citizenry.

We are mostly the same people as we were a decade ago, but it seems like we are now World's away with the changes happening in just a few years. As a people, we resist change as part of our nature. I don't know how we have changed so much in less than a decade. From politics to trusting our government and even to our neighbors, trust has been diminished.

Pew Research has some of the best statistics on how and when disillusioned Americans started distrusting their own government. How long have other world communities distrusted us as a nation? It is simple, for forever!

Why would other communities trust our leaders? It seems daily the social media and the mass media have found our leadership has been lying to their own electorate. Elected leaders have found that it is easier to lie than work on giving the truth. The truth is sometimes hard and mostly difficult to manage. A good example of this happened recently. A northern, Red state municipality had their water supplies polluted with all sorts of contaminants. It was easier to blame previous administrations and diverted the issue of unclean water going to the jurisdictional residents. What could have worked was to say we are working on finding a solution, and then do it. Then give updates even if you are politically damaged. Give respect to the people who gave you that position of authority, and only give them the truth. Overall, disillusioned residents were hurt by these political figures that were supposed to care for them for months.

President Carter gave us the excuse for Americans not to trust the government. He explained in his Malaise speech, we as Americans shouldn't expect to live so well in the world. At this time when political strongmen, hyper-nationalism, and xenophobia had risen in the U.S. and the world.

Carter's speech offers us as Americans a pitiful counterexample to these trends.

Disillusionment in America always follows weak presidents like Carter. Being opposite of Carter made Reagan shine like the sun. But how fast it grows is a product of the media. People from around the world know about each circumstance and digression in American politics. Politics has become the new sports event. Sides are taken, right or left, people choose to watch more of what was considered sleazy and inhibited a decade ago. People fall into the grip of watching a tragic event unfold like Soaps were watched in the daytime hours by housewives. No community is safe. It can change though. We will have to trust that a single problem, and poli-

ticians pushed it to a "back burner", won't turn into a leadership ideology.

*An uncertain world is certain because of a lack of truth
exhibited by our elected leaders...*

First our hearts are broken, it becomes a distrust in everything that stems from our governmental legislative and the
executive branches of government. Problem-solving becomes even greater. No one will want to listen to ideas com-
ing from someone that doesn't have your trust already. Look
at Obama's favorite quote about his healthcare debacle. "If
you like your doctor, you can keep your doctor". After what
happened after those words were spoken became falsities.
No one wanted this system after they found out that their
premiums were doubled and tripped because the government needs that extra money from you to pay for someone
else's healthcare.

Moreover, each party carries its distinct ideology, not trusting
anyone without the same ideals. Everyone had real issues
with the party of Obama and Clinton. Americans of working
age and in their prime earning capacities knew this new tax
would destroy their families. So that "taxation", without repre-
sentation, was hardest on families with careers. Now, younger people are full of that: "the government is here to help
everyone's thought process", knowing that this President is
doing great things for the less fortunate Americans. Now a
decade after, this tax is still being felt by the younger people
in the US. Blooming careerists see their paychecks dwindle
because the government can't stop the free giveaways after
they start them. Just like President Truman's Social Security
system and President Johnson's Medicaid programs, they
can't now be dismantled. It always seems like one party
loves giving away taxpayers money to anyone else from the
same political party. Is this protecting your voters or a payoff
for voting for this political class?

Distrust rapidly becomes the commonality between each ideology. As one side of the political hierarchy sees the other gain momentum in gaining a new voting block, they try to create the same effects using their social mechanism. The policies that drive distrust are what gives the 24/7 media outlets pleasure. The media will love to boost one ideology over the other one. Just as CNN was known as the Clinton News Network because they covered that president's ideology to the grave. CNN news reporters have recently been replaced with storytellers that always slant stories against one party over the other. Always taking the side of the Democratic Party has made this left leaning media out the most biased organization on TV. Once you know they can only see one side of every story's ideology, no one ever trusts them to tell us the truth as a nation.

What did the Clinton Presidency run into that slowed this Progressive president?

Congress took several major actions to oppose or constrain the Clinton administration:

Impeachment Proceedings: In 1998, the House of Representatives impeached President Clinton on charges of perjury and obstruction of justice related to his testimony about the Monica Lewinsky affair. The House adopted two articles of impeachment, but the Senate ultimately acquitted Clinton, allowing him to remain in office.

Government Shutdowns: After Republicans took control of Congress in 1994, budget conflicts with Clinton led to two major government shutdowns in 1995-1996. The shutdowns occurred because Clinton vetoed Republican budget proposals that included deep spending cuts, especially to Medicare and social programs, and tax cuts for the wealthy. The standoff ended when Congress accepted a compromise closer to Clinton's position.

Blocking Legislation: Congress refused to act on several Clinton initiatives, most notably his ambitious health care reform plan in 1994, which failed to gain enough support to pass.

Defeating Stimulus Proposals: In 1993, Republicans in the Senate filibustered and ultimately defeated Clinton's economic stimulus package, allowing only extended unemployment compensation to pass.

Administrative Limits: Congress also passed legislation to create the National Nuclear Security Administration (NNSA), despite opposition from Clinton. Clinton attempted to circumvent the law after signing it, prompting congressional outrage and hearings, though Congress had limited recourse beyond expressing disapproval.

These actions illustrate how Congress, particularly when controlled by the opposition party, used its legislative and oversight powers to challenge and limit the Clinton administration's agenda.

The Republican Congress's budget proposals in the mid-1990s differed sharply from President Clinton's in several key areas:

Spending Cuts vs. Program Protection: Republicans proposed deep cuts—about $433 billion over seven years—to Medicare and Medicaid, as well as significant reductions in education, environmental protection, and other social programs. Clinton opposed these cuts, arguing they would harm seniors, children, and working families, and insisted on protecting these programs.

Tax Policy: The Republican budget included substantial tax cuts, with nearly half of the benefits going to the wealthiest Americans. Clinton objected, saying these cuts were excessive and primarily benefited the rich at the expense of vital services.

Approach to Balancing the Budget: While both sides agreed on the goal of balancing the budget, Republicans aimed for a balanced budget in seven years through aggressive spending cuts. Clinton favored a more gradual approach, balancing the budget without deep cuts to core social programs.

Other Differences: The Republican budget also included provisions to open the Arctic National Wildlife Refuge to oil drilling and allowed corporations more leeway to raid pension funds, both of which Clinton opposed.

In summary, the Republican Congress prioritized rapid deficit reduction through spending cuts and tax breaks, while Clinton sought to balance the budget with fewer cuts to social programs and less emphasis on tax reductions for the wealthy.

The Clinton administration's economic policies had several major consequences:

Economic Growth and Job Creation: The U.S. experienced its longest peacetime economic expansion, with real GDP growing at an average of 3.8% annually and the creation of about 22 million new jobs. Unemployment dropped to its lowest levels in over 30 years, and inflation remained low.

Deficit Reduction and Surpluses: Clinton's focus on fiscal discipline—raising taxes on higher incomes, cutting spending, and expanding the Earned Income Tax Credit—reduced the federal deficit from $290 billion in 1992 to budget surpluses from 1998 to 2001, the first surpluses since 1969.

Rising Wages and Productivity: Real wages began to rise across the economic spectrum, and productivity growth nearly doubled compared to the previous two decades.

Trade and Globalization: Clinton championed free trade agreements like NAFTA and supported China's entry into the WTO, which increased trade but also contributed to a sharp rise in the U.S. trade deficit and concerns about job losses in manufacturing.

Financial Deregulation: Deregulatory measures, such as the Gramm–Leach–Bliley Act, are criticized for contributing to financial instability and laying groundwork for the later Great Recession.

Criticism and Long-Term Risks: While the economy boomed, critics argue that Clinton's policies contributed to rising income inequality and did not sufficiently protect labor rights. The late 1990s also saw the growth of speculative bubbles and a surging current account deficit, raising concerns about the sustainability of the expansion.

In summary, Clinton's actions led to robust economic performance and fiscal improvement in the short term, but some policies—especially on trade and financial deregulation—had mixed long-term effects.

The main criticisms of the Clinton administration's economic policies include:

Financial Deregulation: Clinton's support for deregulating the financial sector—such as the repeal of the Glass-Steagall Act and the Commodity Futures Modernization Act—has been widely criticized for contributing to the conditions that led to the 2008 financial crisis.

Income Inequality: Critics argue Clinton did not do enough to address rising income and wealth inequality. His policies are seen as failing to reverse or even exacerbating trends toward greater inequality that began in previous decades.

Welfare Reform: The 1996 welfare reform law dramatically reduced welfare rolls, but critics say it weakened the social safety net and left the most vulnerable Americans with insufficient support, especially during economic downturns.

Free Trade Agreements: Clinton's championing of NAFTA and support for China's entry into the WTO are blamed for accelerating the loss of U.S. manufacturing jobs and contributing to deindustrialization and wage stagnation for some workers.

Neglect of Labor and Social Security: Clinton was criticized for not strengthening union rights or collective bargaining and for failing to address long-term challenges to Social Security and Medicare, leaving these programs unreformed as the Baby Boom generation approached retirement.

Environmental Concerns: Some policies, such as NAFTA and logging measures, were seen as compromising environmental standards for economic gains.

Education Reform: Clinton's education initiatives, like the Goals 2000 program, were criticized for inconsistent results and failing to equalize standards nationwide.

Attribution of Economic Boom: Some argue Clinton received too much credit for the 1990s economic boom, which they attribute to factors like the tech bubble, per-existing growth trends, and actions by the Republican-controlled Congress.

Overall, while Clinton presided over strong economic growth, critics from both the left and right contend that his policies contributed to later financial instability, rising inequality, and insufficient protection for vulnerable populations.

During the Clinton administration, Republicans took several actions to oppose Clinton's policies and advance their own agenda, especially after gaining control of Congress in the 1994 midterm elections.

Key Republican Actions:

Government Shutdowns (1995-1996): Republicans, led by Speaker Newt Gingrich, demanded major spending cuts, tax reductions, and changes to Medicare and Medicaid. When Clinton refused to sign their budget proposals, this led to two federal government shutdowns. Ultimately, public backlash forced Republicans to compromise and accept Clinton's budget.

Blocking Legislation: Throughout Clinton's presidency, solid Republican opposition in Congress made it difficult for him to pass many of his initiatives, including health care reform and campaign finance reform. This opposition limited Clinton's ability to enact his full agenda and forced him to adopt more centrist positions.

Welfare Reform: Republicans pushed for welfare reform, and after prolonged negotiations, Clinton signed the Personal Responsibility and Work Opportunity Reconciliation Act in 1996, which imposed work requirements and time limits on welfare benefits.

Investigations and Scandals: Republicans supported and amplified investigations into Clinton's personal and professional conduct, including the Whitewater affair and other controversies, keeping the administration on the defensive.

Efforts to Eliminate Federal Departments: Republicans proposed eliminating certain federal agencies, such as the Department of Commerce, which Clinton attributed partly to political and racial motivations.

Impact on America:

These actions contributed to a period of divided government, forcing compromise and sometimes gridlock.

Some Republican-led initiatives, like welfare reform, had lasting impacts on federal policy.

The government shutdowns hurt the Republican image with the public, helping Clinton regain political strength and popularity.

Overall, Republicans sought to restrain government spending, reduce the size of government, and counter Clinton's policies, but public backlash to some of their tactics led to mixed results and required both sides to find middle ground.

People are not surprised with the government's overreach...
Government overreach means this can occur when it acts arbitrarily or invades individual life, liberty, or property.

Our constitution was written to protect us from all these examples that have recently occurred.

The Biden Administration proposed more than $2 trillion in new overreaching and burdensome regulations that President Trump partially degraded or cleaned out completely.

Government intervention in higher education constrains the freedom of inquiry and expression...

Obama's overreaching rule giving the federal government the authority to regulate over 99% of the land in Missouri. The Federal government overreaching in local elections is redefining voting blocks within a state.

Due process can protect individuals from government over-reach. Due process ensures that the government provides procedural safeguards before it can invade individual life, liberty, or property. Our Bill of Rights and the 10th amendment takes care of many privacy issues not stated within the Constitution. That means litigation. Courts are deciding on everyday issues that curtail Americans rights. Some businesses are as well. Small businesses are the worst hit by regulations because they can't afford lawyers to fight so many regulative laws.

Ever since England's Magna Carta - which limited the King's power over the citizens, humans have had a desire to lead their own lives, the way that they want, without a government telling them how to do it. Governments also hold fiscal controls over its peoples. It has been known that government interventions in the economy can distort national markets and reduce competition, resulting in shortages or high prices. The way the government is supposed to work is to protect its citizenry, not overprotect. It is like describing heaven and hell. Enough is sometimes right, and for others it is too much. Look at Sweden and other socialist societies. They love having the government tell them how to live and what they should pay for. As Americans we could never imagine a self-reliant lifestyle following that model of living. An Independent nature is what has built America into the greatest nation this world has ever seen. Others think that this heavenly statement is more hellish.

Limiting government is the ideal heaven that is always on the lips of many that say it is really hell. As a lifelong believer in limited government, that should be our goal every time an election happens. We were as Independent to limit the Feds reach, as other countries like Ireland, we might be able to do better in business with other countries. The Feds hold our ability to bring business here by the way of taxation. Another stumbling block for Democratic leaders. If businesses see you are hurting them with taxes, they won't come here to do business. When they establish a presence here they hire Americans, and they pay wage taxes also. The businesses pay taxes when they operate here, if they are lower they are more likely to build more business situations here in America. As the coffers fill, what matters is who is filling them, the extra people that are employed or more businesses start because of lesser regulations and lower taxation rate.

Highly regulated countries are never ones that succeed in creating more money from taxes. The companies you require to pay more will just get up, leave for a place they feel safe and wanted, like Ireland. So the business doesn't hire the Americans they need for the business, and the populous suffers because the government was greedily increasing the taxes on a going company to pay for all the social programs that have drained America's ability to sustain itself with borrowing. The government with its over regulation and constant never ending spending on unnecessary programs have made the US a place that business will not go, even for a better workforce.

Everyone expects not to believe what their governments are telling them.

The Republican Party has employed a variety of strategies and tactics to counter what they perceive as leftist attacks on American values, institutions, and policies. These efforts have included legislative actions, public messaging, and grassroots organizing. Here are some key ways in which Republicans have sought to block or counter these perceived attacks:

Legislative Measures:
 Tax Cuts: Republicans often advocate for tax cuts and deregulation as a means to promote economic growth, which they argue counters the left's approach to larger government and higher taxes.

 Healthcare: Efforts to repeal or modify the Affordable Care Act (Obamacare) have been a central focus, with Republicans arguing that it leads to government overreach in healthcare.

 Education: Promoting school choice and opposing critical race theory and other progressive educational reforms is another strategy used to counter what they see as leftist influence in education.

Messaging and Rhetoric: Republicans frequently frame their opposition to leftist policies as a defense of American values, emphasizing themes like individual liberty, personal responsibility, and free enterprise.
  - They use social media and other platforms to amplify their messages, often portraying leftist policies as extreme or un-American.

Judicial Appointments: The appointment of conservative judges to federal courts, including the Supreme Court, has been a significant Republican strategy to influence legal interpretations of laws and rights in favor of conservative principles.

Grassroots Organizing: The Republican Party and affiliated organizations often mobilize grassroots supporters to advocate for conservative policies at local, state, and national levels. This includes rallies, town halls, and community engagement efforts.

*Cultural and Social Advocacy**:* Republicans often engage in cultural debates, seeking to push back against progressive movements in areas such as gender identity, abortion, and gun rights. They emphasize traditional family values and religious freedoms in their messaging.

*Countering Media Narratives**:* The rise of conservative media platforms has allowed Republicans to challenge mainstream narratives and present alternative viewpoints to counter perceived bias in liberal media.

*Electoral Strategy**:* Focusing on winning elections at all levels—federal, state, and local—allows Republicans to block leftist initiatives by gaining control over legislative bodies and governorships.

These strategies are part of an ongoing political battle in the United States, where both parties seek to promote their respective visions for the country. The effectiveness of these strategies can vary significantly depending on the political climate and the issues at stake.

Republicans often argue that their policies safeguard fiscal responsibility, promote individual liberties, and protect traditional social values, which they believe counterbalance what they perceive as excessive government intervention and progressive social policies from the left. By advocating for lower taxes, deregulation, and a strong national defense, they contend that these strategies stimulate economic growth, preserve personal freedoms, and maintain national security, ultimately positioning themselves as defenders of individual rights and stability in the face of what they view as leftist overreach.

Since the time of Kennedy's presidency, polls have consistently told us that Americans don't believe our government. One shoe after another drops, and our belief in the Federal government shrinks. Kennedy had Cuban controversy, hiding the facts of a secret failed invasion. There was Watergate for Nixon. Carter has the hostages and oil prices. Clinton had his trial where he was found guilty of lying to Congress and his hands were tied for the rest of his years in office. Bush had 911 and an economy that was hobbling into recession.

Obama had overreaching regulations mandating each person in the US had to pay for someone else's healthcare cost. This all has led to 23% of Democratic Party voters believing in their government and 8% for Republicans. Many people say the government is doing too much in the way of restricting American businesses. Younger adults are leading the polls on this.

Americans think the publics trust has been in decline for both the Federal government (64% distrust) and their neighbors.

Neighbors and neighboring countries think the same. Who is there to trust with the lives of your family on the balance? 69% of Americans say the Federal Government withholds information from them. Worldwide organizations are forming World Courts to develop rules on how to conduct your lives. Those laws would not be reversible for Americans. We are being asked to conform to silly standards like air and water quality when the largest polluters are not being mandated to do so. There are emission standards going in place that will take away the freedoms of Americans from owning and driving their favorite gas propelled vehicles. Some countries are asking for reductions around the world in carbon emissions to help in climate change, but the worst polluters, like China and India, have special carve outs to limit their restrictions.

The WHO (World Health Organization) is one of the conspirators of the ultimate spread of the China virus in the world. Their suggested regulations stopped many countries from having any economic activity for two years.

Also creating and allowing dictatorships to help halt the spread of a virus with little reasoning. They lied their way through bureaucracies across our world to make their power grab inevitable and absolute.

Looks like our future is filled with elitists Governing us towards turns socialist tendencies and they are mandated to soon be permanent as directed by a one party rule as its goal.

National Politics Now:
Not since the Civil War a century and a half ago has the United States been so divided. A surprising number of Americans on both sides of the political divide talk of another civil war. Certainly, the nation is involved in a cultural civil war and has been for quite some time.

Biden spoke of unity in his Inaugural Address, using the word nine times and urging his fellow Americans 'to see each other not as adversaries but as neighbors [and] . . . treat each other with dignity and respect'. Fine words indeed. But despite calling himself 'the unifier in chief', he has done nothing but further divide the American people since taking office, demoralizing those who oppose his destructive policies and labeling those who voted for Trump in 2020 (just over 74 million Americans) 'a threat to democracy'.

President Biden has been a unifier, he has unified most Americans against him and his policies.

Biden revealed his hand that he was going to be the worst President in 60 years when he awarded the Presidential

Medal of Freedom—the highest civilian honor—to George Soros, the man who launched and helped fund the soft-on-crime "rogue prosecutor" movement.

- Due to Soros' advocacy, prosecutors across the country routinely ignore certain crimes, enabling lawlessness.

Yet, Biden considered Soros an American hero because of his "philanthropy" to "strengthen weakened democracy, left-wing human rights, social engineering rather than the education of how social justice weekend the American meritocracy.

George Soros founded the Open Society Foundations, and its money fuels the broader engine of woke activist groups that advised the administrative state under Biden.

These activists support a constellation of liberal issues that I summarize with the term "*woke*," from critical race theory (the notion that America is systemically racist in favor of whites and against blacks, a notion driving efforts for "diversity, equity, and inclusion"), to gender ideology (the notion that an internal sense of "gender identity" overrides biological sex), to climate alarmism (the belief that human burning of fossil fuels is destroying the earth), to a preference for technocratic government by experts rather than by elected representatives.

Upwards of 70% of most polls taken says he should be removed from high office. Even in his strongest holdover cities, they are backing away their support for him. His press conference all but proves he is cognitively impaired. He should not be allowed to say he is a leader that will bring America back together. Straight fairy tails are being uttered from the podium on a daily basis. He has recently admitted he was wrong about stopping construction on the Southern border wall, more than 9 million illegal criminals crossing our non-existent border.

How he has demonized the other half of this nation is not a political aspiration, it is a death knell in the coffin of his Presidency. Unifiers do not tell their followers that the other political party is evil and is filled with bad citizens. This is an amateurish trick used by the now discredited and mistrusted Hillary Clinton. Her followers have dropped off that bandwagon half a decade ago.

The New York Times has even stated that 67% of America distrusts her. She is the real result of having unlimited governmental power. Everyone thought Nixon took advantage of his kingly position. He is an amateur compared to her.

The Clinton's and their admirers have brought this country to a standstill multiple times. During President Clinton's time in office, the US House of Representatives had to put in check his troubled policies.

What about Hillary Clinton?
Hillary has taken what should have been clearly seen as a lie and made the US government stop and hold months of useless trials based upon made up lies from the Clinton campaign. Having the Benghazi issues follow her where she goes has made America distrust her worthiness as a leader. She doesn't see herself as being subject to the same laws that all other Americans have to live within. The worst of all, after being discredited so much the past decade, she still is considering running again for the Presidency because Biden is so horrific.

Hillary Clinton has faced numerous allegations of "cover-ups" throughout her public career, often tied to major controversies and scandals. The most prominent include:
Email Controversy: As Secretary of State, Clinton used a private email server for official business. Critics accused her of trying to hide communications from public scrutiny and mishandling classified information. The FBI concluded she was

"extremely careless" but recommended no criminal charges, and multiple investigations found no intent to break the law. The controversy, however, dominated media coverage and damaged her public image.

Benghazi Attack: Clinton was accused by political opponents of covering up details about the 2012 attack on the U.S. mission in Benghazi, Libya, which killed four Americans. Several congressional investigations found no evidence of criminal wrongdoing or a deliberate cover-up, though Clinton accepted responsibility for security lapses.

Whitewater and Related Scandals: The Whitewater investigation centered on the Clintons' real estate investments and raised questions about Hillary Clinton's legal work and the disappearance of related documents. After years of probes, no charges were filed against her, but critics alleged she was not fully transparent.

Clinton Foundation: Allegations surfaced that Clinton used her influence to benefit donors to the Clinton Foundation. No direct evidence of a criminal cover-up was found, but questions about transparency and conflicts of interest persisted.

While these controversies fueled accusations of cover-ups, official investigations generally did not result in criminal charges against Clinton. Nonetheless, the perception of secrecy and defensiveness contributed to public mistrust and became a recurring theme in her political career.

The way the world saw here was through the
lens of the media..

The media's portrayal of Hillary Clinton's denials evolved from early skepticism and persistent negativity to a more entrenched narrative of untrustworthiness, shaped by both partisan and mainstream outlets:

Early Coverage: In the 1990s and early 2000s, media coverage often focused on Clinton's refusal to conform to traditional gender roles, criticizing her for being outspoken or ambitious. Negative framing was common whenever she did not fit expected roles, such as the backlash over her "baking cookies" comment.

Scandal and Suspicion: As controversies like Whitewater, Benghazi, and especially the email server emerged, media outlets increasingly framed Clinton's denials as evasive or insincere. Conservative media, in particular, amplified allegations of dishonesty, while mainstream outlets often repeated these themes, reinforcing a narrative of suspicion and character flaws.

2016 Election Cycle: During her presidential campaign, the negativity intensified. Studies found that Clinton received overwhelmingly negative coverage, with stories about her alleged dishonesty outpacing positive press by a wide margin. The media frequently recycled old accusations and rarely contextualized her denials or the outcomes of investigations, making "Clinton lied" a dominant storyline.

Persistent Narrative: Even as fact-checkers and some journalists concluded she was "fundamentally honest," these findings struggled to gain traction. The press often relied on speculation and repeated unproven claims, contributing to a persistent public perception of untrustworthiness and holding her to higher standards than male counterparts.

Over time, the media's portrayal of Clinton's denials became less about the specifics of each case and more about reinforcing a broader, negative narrative—one that often overshadowed factual outcomes and shaped lasting public skepticism.

Hillary Clinton's team used several strategies to influence the media narrative and counter negative coverage:

Building Relationships with Reporters: Clinton's aides, including John Podesta and Joel Benenson, hosted private dinners and outreach events with campaign reporters and TV anchors to build rapport and encourage more favorable or balanced coverage.

Rapid Response and Media Monitoring: Organizations like Media Matters for America, closely aligned with Clinton allies, actively monitored press coverage and pushed back against negative stories, aiming to correct misinformation and challenge unfavorable narratives in real time.

Strategic Messaging and Offensive Tactics: The campaign sought to "wrest control of the narrative" by going on the offensive—promoting Clinton's key policy ideas, highlighting her rationale for running, and targeting specific reporters and outlets that showed interest in her campaign's message.

Defensive Posture and Narrative Reset: During periods of intense scrutiny, such as the email controversy, the team worked to reset relations with the press and shift the focus from scandals to Clinton's qualifications and policy agenda, acknowledging the need for a better relationship with the media.

Counteracting Right-Wing Narratives: Clinton's team and supportive media activists worked to expose and counteract coordinated right-wing messaging campaigns that injected negative stories into mainstream coverage, recognizing the influence of partisan media ecosystems on broader public perception.

These efforts reflected a blend of behind-the-scenes relationship-building, public messaging campaigns, and rapid response operations designed to shape how Clinton was portrayed in the media.

This affliction she has with her self-importance probably festered during the FBI's pseudo-investigation on her about her lack of importance about pertinent server security. It was judged by same-team lawmakers that her actions, although illegal, didn't come to a threshold for a trial and punishment. She deflected the obvious illegal activities just long enough for the Trump charges to take hold of the news cycle. Even though she was judged by others involved in the "Deep-state", the American people saw the truth. She was untouchable because of who she was and a former head of state. President Trump tells the US the Deep-state was a group of influencing political or military officials who were involved in secret manipulation of our governing policy.

What have politics gave us as under a Biden Presidency?
President Biden promised so much to Americans there was no way they ever expected any of them to work.

Now that everyone can feel Disillusionment in this Biden-Harris Presidency, we are now waiting to see the pivot most elected officials do when their likability ratings drop into the cellar. He hasn't pivoted like previous administrations so we can expect that his promises will disappear as fast as they can make up a cover story. His use of executive authority has not been checked by the other branches of government so it looks as though these final months of this administration will be concerned more with deflecting questions more than they usually do.

His work for the final months looks as though they might include some kind of a legacy protecting win. He had advocated for Medicare for all but that has been dropped.

He was all in for affordable medicines stating it could be the most important factor in curtaining COVID and its historic chronic nature, yet nothing. He could not even give us better pricing on medicinal drugs. He tried to get a national $15.00 an hour minimum wage passed but, nothing. He said he was going to halt drilling for oil but as the prices of gasoline doubled and tripled in the country he had to flip flop. He could have let the Pipeline be built pumping 600,000 barrels a day into America but he canceled them and decided to back natural gas. He tried to give away other taxpayers money to cancel debt on those going to college and never was able to get that passed. He has always hung his hat on being a Union supportive President, he gave Amazon $10 billion while that company caught labor organizing. Most of his actions have been counterproductive for Americans. His commitment to big corporations and other governments has been concerning for voters. His falling approval ratings have proven he can not dig his way out of this Malaise.

What has this begot to Politics:
> *We can congratulate President Trump in uncovering and repeatedly telling the story about the deep-state.*
> *The deep state has its roots in the government because of Operation Paperclip.*

President Trump easily exposed our government colluding with big tech to suppress stories that didn't benefit the parties of the deep-state. It became a daily news story in America. On the scale of any part of the Watergate debacle, it was shown that our nation was now being ruled by politicians deeply rooted in the system of government and elitists of our tech companies.

Everyone remembers how the big tech giant Twitter deplatformed a President but allowed a terrorist organization to use their platform to spread their lies to the world. Now we see, big tech is protecting the Presidency of Joe Biden by not allowing the flow of discrediting information to flow out to the American public. Big Tech has also organized a silencing of conservative voices speaking to the origins of the COVID virus. People are still reeling from the disinformation the deep state used to get American to conform to the new rules of getting the jab. Over and over again, the government acts to protect themselves and the elites within its circle.

Monopoly Power of the Swamp Is Crushing America. Washington is filled with players in a corrupt monopoly system. The system (the Swamp) benefits the connected citizens and companies espousing a certain belief. There is a power surge stemming from Washington (our largest monopoly) and going into silicon valleys back yards. Silicon Valley (the next largest monopoly) has been the place where massive concentration of economic power in the technology, financial, and media industries, over the last forty years, has had both an economic and a sacred demand on American people. These powerful groups of like minded bureaucratic and techies have done more to damage Americans by being capable of predetermining a wage barrier that won't let wages accelerate naturally stemming from competition.

This immunity from government is the biggest reason how these companies have prospered as typical Americans see diminished value and benefits in their lives. Americans have been frustrated by these supposed representative delegates Over the decades. As you know, that's why we have elections. If you want a change in the way you are represented in the government, change your representative by voting them out of the office. Getting to the point when you think your vote doesn't make a change then you need to not complain about the situation you are now living in. Only a government of the people and by the people can be changed.

Antitrust regulations should be something American can vote on as well. Antitrust laws are there to break up monopolies, and if the government is one of the monopolies then vote differently. Monopolies have been in existence forever, but when the government gets in on it, then the American people fail. We need less big business and government working together because when they do the family's economy goes downward. Without businesses competing for employees wages never rise. The government telling business there is a national minimum wage is crazy. There is such a living wage difference when you live and work in New York compared to a place like any small town in Alabama. Wages should reflect regional terms and levels. Government's interference doesn't allow for this. If the tech companies in Silicon Valley say that an entry level position should only pay $40 a hour, then the rest of the country will average about the same for that job title.

The feeling of powerlessness is held by those trapped in this regulated system. Government does help but as they do, they entrench themselves into your lives. Always there as a deterrent for you to do better in most cases.

They are always looking for ways to get a play to pay leverage on your family.

The last Decades and our Economic Malaise...

Interestingly, today, even though people are feeling negative about the future, their spending on necessities and substance hasn't been affected. The Economist publication says that "actions matter more than the truth of numbers when it comes down to the economy." A rise in or a steady path upward in consumer spending indeed always drives the perception of a strong economy. Lately, negative consumer attitudes don't equal an economic down click, as it would have in the past. Today's economy is perception based. If it looks as though you are doing well, even if you are still struggling to keep away from the bill collector, you are perceived to be a success. In the suburb areas of the US, everyone buys that fantastic house in a great neighborhood but its mortgage cost is so high every month you can afford to furnish the inside.

Many Americans seem to have a gloomy mood when it comes to their personnel finances. It implies to be the norm across age groups. The pandemic has contributed to this, in a way that was unexpected. In broader social and cultural factors, it has prevented more people from going to a daily place of work. This isolates us but has also freed many Americans to pursue a better way of life because working at home has become the norm. Individualistically, it has led people to distrust the previous conviction of having to commute to work. The stress lost just in this has people aiming for a better job that limits going to a physical place of work. Of course, the Business districts are all now suffering. The businesses that support a busy downtown district are too seeing downturns. A Malaise in the metropolitan eateries in city centers might be the hardest hit sector of the economy. All these occurrences are lessening the need to hold steady physical business locations. As work profiles change and people realize they aren't necessary, outsourcing might make this goal of not going into a place of work destroy the single best thing about being this free.

Outsourcing of common office jobs might be the new Malaise we will have brought onto ourselves. In 2023, the situation is similar to the "malaise" experienced during Jimmy Carter's presidency in the late 1970s. Americans are struggling to improve their lives by not having to physically go to an office. So that means the office can be anywhere on the Internet cloud. This will lead to persistent inflation and stagnant wages in these non office based communities. Because, there will always be someone in a mediocre currency-based country willing to do work from the cloud - based office to get a substantially higher wage than what they could have reaped in their native lands.

The cost of everyday items keeps increasing, to make up for lagging sales in a marketplace, making it harder for people to make it past this new outsourcing trend.

Of course, being the innovator in so many common luxuries has made Americans and businesses strong in ways our ancestors never could have dreamed. Our modern conveniences that are thought of as necessities by Americans, like air conditioning, heating, refrigeration, and microwaves, are yet to be commonplace in countries around the world. These typical examples have driven the economies of the US and made these conditions into business necessities just to be a viable workplace. In other countries, they can undercut American business costs in order to save money in doing business with these foreign offices. This will not improve our lives. These innovations not only make us more comfortable and convenient to our daily workplace lives yet it will soon be gone as well because business always looks for ways to save money in doing business and the costs that are involved.

Similar to the days of Carter....
America's current problems can be traced back to excessive government spending in giving subsidies to Americans not to work. The pandemic has proven that when people have the choice to stay at home, they will. Americans getting paid not to work will have bad results.

The Federal Reserves attempts to stabilize the pandemics economic downtown by printing more money and distributing it through social services will devalue the dollar that is currently being used. This of course will drive prices higher because when the value of a product remains the same in the purchaser's mind, the only difference is how much it will cost with a devalued dollar. People don't seem to complain that a dozen eggs cost $6.00 now after the pandemic. Soon it will be causally named the Biden economy. This is what generations of Americans have called a worsening of the Economy.

"Capitalism" with a large C, can be in and out of fashion....
Since the 1980s, it has become the sign of America's success. Americans support the idea of a free market and let things cost whatever someone is willing to pay for them.
As the government interviews and tries to level the playing field for all Americans, it counteracts the process. Allowing innovators to create tools to be successful, they should be rewarded with the ability to charge what they need to cover the costs of invention and production. Innovations make Capitalism sing. Capitalism enhances our lives and allows the innovator to enjoy the rewards of their hard work. When the government takes the process over, a Malaise will soon follow.

The 1990s were the threshold that made America once again a powerhouse economy. Despite the government's Malaise in previous decades, Reagan economic ideals made the stock market (our way to measure the economy's progress) double before he left office and set it trending skywards ever since.

What America needs is someone who can lift the spirits of the nation and restore our hope. We need a leader who can replace Joe Biden and inspire the public to embrace the American uplifting ways of previous resurgences. This reestablished pride in doing well for all Americans can be seen in President Trump. An accomplishment like this after a Biden White house will require electing a leader who is authentic, yet also a skilled rhetorician (sound familiar). Throughout American history, such leaders have always emerged at our darkest hour. President Reagan, are you listening? Send us a Liberator and protector such as yourself.

Chapter Seven:
Malaise comparison Carter vs. Biden:

A Comparative Analysis of Economic Conditions and Public Sentiment: The "Biden Malaise" and the Carter Administration.

Summary of Similarities:

This report compares economic conditions and public sentiment during the "Biden malaise" and Jimmy Carter's presidency. The term "Biden malaise" has recently emerged in discussions, particularly among conservatives, implying a resemblance to the economic challenges confronted by Carter's administration. While both periods experienced significant economic difficulties and public dissatisfaction, this analysis identifies significant differences in economic indicators, underlying causes of the challenges, and policy responses implemented. Key findings show that, while inflation was a major concern in both eras, unemployment was significantly higher under Carter. Carter, while GDP growth exhibited comparable averages. The causes of the economic downturns differed, with Carter dealing with external oil shocks and pre-existing stagflation, and Biden dealing with the unprecedented disruptions of a global pandemic and its aftermath. Policy responses also differed, reflecting the unique challenges of each period. Finally, while the term "Biden malaise" evokes a sense of public unease reminiscent of the late 1970s, a closer examination of the economic data and historical context reveals a more nuanced picture, cautioning against oversimplification of these two distinct periods in American economic history.

Intro...

The term "Biden malaise" has entered the political and economic lexicon, with commentators frequently drawing parallels between the current economic climate under President Joe Biden and President Jimmy Carter's struggles in the late

1970s. This analogy suggests a period marked by economic stagnation, high inflation, and a general sense of national unease. This comparison is critical for understanding the historical context of today's economic challenges, as well as identifying potential lessons that can be applied to current policymaking and political discourse. This report seeks to provide a thorough examination of the similarities and differences between these two periods. It will look at the definition of "Biden malaise," key economic indicators like inflation, unemployment, and GDP growth during both eras, the primary causes and contributing factors to the economic difficulties, the policy responses implemented by both administrations, and finally, public sentiment and approval ratings related to the economy. The report's detailed comparison aims to provide a more nuanced understanding of the economic and political realities of both the Carter administration and today.

Defining "Biden Malaise:
In its broadest sense, the term "malaise" refers to an indefinite sense of weakness or ill health that is frequently preceded by illness. It can also describe a general state of mental or moral distress. Because of this inherent vagueness, the term can be applied broadly to periods of societal discontent that are not solely defined by quantifiable metrics. Kimberley Strassel's book "The Biden Malaise: How America Bounces Back from Joe Biden's Dismal Repeat of the Jimmy Carter Years" has had a significant impact on current usage of the term "Biden malaise." This book is a foundational text for understanding the term as it is currently used in political discourse, particularly in conservative media and commentary. Strassel contends that President Biden's tenure mirrors the perceived failures of Jimmy Carter's presidency, claiming that both leaders have engulfed the country in "weakness, inflation, and political unrest." Strassel's comparison highlights specific economic issues such as "soaring energy prices and inflation." Beyond these economic factors, Strassel sees broader parallels in "domestic and foreign policy morasses" and a pervasive "national ennui" that she claims both the

Carter and Biden administrations experienced. Strassel also claims that President Biden's situation is "ultimately far worse" than Carter's, primarily because she believes Biden "inherited a better situation" but "doubled down on Carter's mistakes." This assertion implies that a significant difference exists between each president's initial economic conditions and subsequent policy decisions. The claim of a "better" inheritance necessitates a thorough examination of the economic indicators at the beginnings of both presidencies, which will be done later in this report. It is important to note that the term "Biden malaise" is primarily critical and politically charged, and is frequently used by conservative commentators to criticize President Biden's record, particularly in economic management. This viewpoint frequently emphasizes negative economic indicators and paints a picture of national decline under Biden, drawing direct and often disparaging parallels to the Carter administration.

In contrast to its current usage, the term "malaise" originated in American political discourse with a speech given by President Jimmy Carter in 1979. While critics quickly dubbed this address the "malaise speech," Carter never used the term. Instead, he spoke about a broader "crisis of confidence" affecting the nation's spirit, will, and unity of purpose. Carter's remarks went beyond purely economic concerns, delving into societal values like "self-indulgence and consumption," as well as a perceived decline in national productivity and savings. He also criticized a government that appeared "incapable of action." As a result, although "Biden malaise" and the original "malaise" speech, as it became known, both allude to a sense of national woe, the perceived causes and extent of that woe seem to be different. Carter's speech addressed a deeper sense of national unease that encompassed moral and spiritual dimensions, while the modern term seems more focused on economic performance and policy failures, frequently viewed through a partisan lens.

The Economic Crisis During Jimmy Carter's Administration: In January 1977, Jimmy Carter took office as president amid a number of serious economic difficulties. A defining characteristic of this period was "stagflation," a rare and economically painful combination of high inflation and high unemployment that defied conventional economic wisdom at the time. This situation was further exacerbated by a severe energy crisis, most notably the 1979 oil shock, which resulted in widespread gasoline shortages, long lines at the pump, and soaring energy prices that rippled throughout the economy. Significant government spending from the Vietnam War and the growth of social programs in the previous decade, a weakening of the U.S. dollar on global markets, and growing competition from foreign economies—especially Japan and Germany—were some of the other factors that contributed to the economic downturn of the Carter years. Carter took over an economy already struggling with the fallout from the Vietnam War and the breakdown of the Bretton Woods system of fixed exchange rates, which made the economic environment especially complicated and difficult for decision-makers.

A more accurate picture of the economic conditions of the era can be obtained by looking at the major economic indicators during Carter's presidency (1977–1981). Inflation was a dominant feature, with rates steadily climbing and reaching double-digit levels. According to the Consumer Price Index for All Urban Consumers (CPI-U), the annual inflation rate was 6.5% in 1977, 7.6% in 1978, 11.3% in 1979, 13.5% in 1980, and 10.3% in 1981. With the inflation rate approaching an annualized 18.2% during the first three months of 1980, the situation was especially dire. This ongoing and rising inflation reduced American households' purchasing power, increased economic uncertainty, and became a major public concern, all of which had an adverse effect on President Carter's approval ratings.

During Carter's presidency, unemployment took on a more complex form. Initially, the unemployment rate declined after Carter took office, falling from 7.1% in 1977 to 6.1% in 1978 and further to 5.8% in 1979. However, as the economic situation worsened and the country entered a recession in 1980, unemployment rose again, reaching 7.1% in 1980. By May 1980, the unemployment rate had climbed to 7.6%. While inflation was the more prominent economic issue, the rising unemployment, particularly as the economy contracted, contributed to the publics economic anxieties and the overall sense of malaise.

During Carter's presidency, GDP growth followed an initial surge before slowing and contracting significantly. The real GDP growth rate stood at 4.6% in 1977 and increased to 5.5% in 1978 before slowing to 3.2% in 1979. In 1980, the economy experienced a recession, with a real GDP contraction of 0.3%. The second quarter of 1980 saw a particularly sharp downturn, with the Gross National Product (GNP) plummeting at an annualized rate of 9.9%. This recession at the end of Carter's term highlighted the severity of the economic crisis and most likely reinforced the publics negative perception of his administration's economic management.

The Economic Landscape of "Biden Malaise":

The period commonly referred to as "Biden malaise" generally spans from mid-2021 onwards, following the initial recovery phase from the COVID-19 pandemic and coinciding with a noticeable increase in inflation. The economic data available for this analysis extends up to March 2025. Examining the key economic indicators from mid-2021 to March 2025 reveals a distinct economic landscape when compared to the Carter years.

Inflation experienced a significant surge starting in mid-2021, reaching levels not witnessed in the United States for several decades. According to the Bureau of Labor Statistics, the annual inflation rate for all items peaked at 9.1% in June 2022. This rapid increase in the cost of living caused considerable financial strain on American households and quickly became a major point of public concern and political contention.

However, following this peak, inflation began to moderate. By March 2025, the annual inflation rate had fallen to 2.4%. This decline in inflation is a key difference from the consistently rising inflation rates that characterized the majority of Carter's presidency.

Unemployment during the "Biden malaise" period has been remarkably low, standing in stark contrast to the higher unemployment rates prevalent during much of the Carter administration. The national unemployment rate remained below 4% for a sustained period, indicating a strong labor market. As of March 2025, the unemployment rate was 4.2, representing a slight increase from the earlier lows but still a historically low figure. This robust labor market is a significant divergence from the economic challenges faced under President Carter.

GDP Growth under President Biden has shown a pattern of strong recovery in the immediate aftermath of the pandemic, followed by more moderate but generally positive growth. The full-year GDP growth for 2024 was reported at 2.8%. However, more recent estimates for the first quarter of 2025 indicate a potential contraction of -2.5% , suggesting a possible economic slowdown. While the overall growth during Biden's term has been generally positive, the recent indication of a potential contraction introduces a note of concern that could contribute to the narrative of "malaise." Nevertheless, the overall growth trajectory has been more consistent than under Carter, whose term ended in a clear recession.

Comparative Analysis of Key Economic Indicators:
To facilitate a direct comparison, the average annual rates

for the key economic indicators during both periods are presented in the following tables.

Carter Administration (1977-1981) | "Biden Malaise" (2021-2024) ...

Inflation Rate (%)   9.84 | compared to: 5.0

Unemployment Rate (%) 6.53   compared to: 3.78

Carter Administration (1977-1980) | "Biden Malaise" (2021-2024) |

GDP Growth (%) 3.25   compared to: 3.3

The data show that, while both periods experienced economic headwinds, the exact combination of these indicators differed significantly. The Carter administration faced significantly higher average inflation and unemployment rates, resulting in the phenomenon of stagflation. In contrast, the "Biden malaise" period has been characterized by a lower average inflation rate and a significantly lower average unemployment rate. The average GDP growth rates for both periods were comparable. This comparison suggests that while both eras presented considerable economic challenges and fostered public unease, the nature of the economic difficulties, particularly in terms of the labor market, was quite different.

Primary Causes and Contributing Factors:

The economic crisis that defined Jimmy Carter's presidency was a complex interplay of both domestic and global factors. A major contributor was the series of external supply shocks, most notably the dramatic increases in oil prices orchestrated by the Organization of Arab Petroleum Exporting Countries (OAPEC) and exacerbated by geopolitical instability in the Middle East. These oil price hikes had a cascading effect throughout the economy, fueling inflation across various sectors. Furthermore, past monetary policy decisions and the collapse of the Bretton Woods system of fixed exchange rates in the early 1970s had already contributed to underlying inflationary pressures and a weakening of the U.S.

dollar. The legacy of substantial government spending on the Vietnam War and the expansion of social programs in the preceding decade under President Lyndon B. Johnson had also built up inflationary pressures within the economy. Compounding these issues was the challenge of "stagflation" itself, a condition of simultaneous high inflation and unemployment that defied the prevailing Keynesian economic theories of the time, making it difficult to implement effective policy responses.

In contrast, the economic landscape of the "Biden malaise" period was largely shaped by the unprecedented global impact of the COVID-19 pandemic. The pandemic triggered massive disruptions to global supply chains, causing shortages of goods and materials and leading to price increases. Shifts in consumer demand, particularly towards goods rather than services during lockdowns, further strained supply chains. In response to the pandemic's economic fallout, the U.S. government implemented substantial fiscal stimulus packages, such as the American Rescue Plan, aimed at supporting individuals, businesses, and the overall economy. While these measures helped to prevent a deeper economic downturn, some economists argue that they also contributed to increased aggregate demand and fueled inflationary pressures. Additionally, the Russian invasion of Ukraine in early 2022 further exacerbated global supply chain issues, particularly in the energy and food markets, leading to significant price increases in these essential sectors. The relative contributions of these demand-side factors (stimulated by fiscal policy) and supply-side constraints (due to the pandemic and geopolitical events) to the surge in inflation remain a subject of ongoing debate among economists.

Policy Responses and Their Impact:
The Carter administration responded to the economic crisis with a multifaceted approach. Initially, the focus was on stimulating the economy and reducing unemployment through measures like the Economic Stimulus Appropriations Act

and the expansion of public service jobs under the Comprehensive Employment and Training Act (CETA). However, as inflation continued to rise, the administration shifted its focus towards combating price increases. This included efforts at deregulation in key industries such as airlines, trucking, and railroads, with the aim of increasing efficiency and fostering price competition. A pivotal moment in Carter's economic policy was the appointment of Paul Volcker as Chairman of the Federal Reserve in 1979. Volcker implemented a series of aggressive monetary policies, involving significant increases in interest rates, to break the inflationary spiral. While these measures were ultimately successful in curbing inflation, they also contributed to a recession in the short term. Additionally, Carter's administration pursued a national energy policy aimed at reducing the nation's dependence on foreign oil through conservation measures, the development of alternative energy sources, and the creation of the Department of Energy. Despite these efforts, Carter faced significant challenges in working with a divided Congress and overcoming political opposition to enact his full agenda.

The Biden administration's policy responses to the economic challenges of its term have also been extensive. A key initial measure was the American Rescue Plan, a large-scale fiscal stimulus package designed to provide relief from the ongoing COVID-19 pandemic and to support economic recovery. This plan included direct payments to individuals, extensions of unemployment benefits, and aid to state and local governments. The administration has also focused on long-term investments aimed at boosting economic growth and competitiveness through legislation such as the Bipartisan Infrastructure Law, the Inflation Reduction Act, and the CHIPS and Science Act. The Inflation Reduction Act, in particular, aims to address climate change, lower healthcare costs, and reduce the federal deficit. The Biden administration has also pursued efforts to lower specific costs for consumers, such as prescription drugs and energy, and has taken action to address issues like "junk fees". Similar to the Carter era, an independent Federal Reserve has played a crucial role in responding to inflation, implementing a series of aggressive interest rate hikes starting in 2022 to cool down the economy and bring prices under control.

Public Sentiment and Approval Ratings:

Public sentiment during Jimmy Carter's presidency was significantly impacted by the worsening economic conditions. Carter's initial approval ratings, which were quite high, declined sharply as the economic crisis deepened and the energy crisis unfolded. Public disapproval was particularly strong concerning his handling of the economy and the energy problem, reflecting widespread frustration with the rising inflation and gasoline shortages. His 1979 speech addressing a "crisis of confidence," often referred to as the "malaise" speech, was largely received negatively by the public and did not improve his standing, with some viewing it as blaming the American people for the nation's problems. Ultimately, the prevailing economic anxieties, particularly the high rate of inflation, played a significant role in Carter's defeat in the 1980 presidential election, underscoring the strong link between economic conditions and political outcomes.

Public sentiment during the "Biden malaise" period has also been notably negative, particularly regarding the economy, despite some positive economic indicators such as low unemployment. President Biden's approval ratings, especially for his handling of the economy, have remained relatively low for much of his term. There appears to be a disconnect between some objective economic data, such as job growth and initially strong GDP growth, and the persistently negative public sentiment about the state of the economy. Continued public concern over inflation, even as the rate has declined from its peak, suggests that the lingering impact of higher prices on the cost of living may be weighing heavily on public perception. Furthermore, there is a significant partisan divide in how Americans view the economy under Biden, with Democrats generally expressing more positive views compared to

Republicans and independents. This suggests that political polarization may also be playing a role in shaping economic perceptions during this period.

In Conclusion:

In comparing the economic conditions and public sentiment during the Carter administration and the "Biden malaise" period, several key similarities and differences emerge. Both eras were marked by significant economic challenges that led to widespread public unease and negatively impacted presidential approval ratings. Inflation was a major concern in both periods, although the average rate was notably higher under Carter. A crucial difference lies in the labor market, with Carter's presidency experiencing significantly higher unemployment rates compared to the relatively low unemployment during the period associated with "Biden malaise." While average GDP growth rates were comparable, the Carter administration ended with a clear recession, whereas the "Biden malaise" period has seen more consistent, though recently potentially slowing, growth.

The underlying causes of the economic difficulties also differed. Carter grappled with external oil shocks and pre-existing stagflation, while Biden faced the unprecedented disruptions of a global pandemic and its aftermath, along with geopolitical events like the war in Ukraine. Policy responses reflected these distinct challenges, with Carter ultimately relying on aggressive monetary tightening to combat entrenched inflation, and Biden initially focusing on large-scale fiscal stimulus followed by support for Federal Reserve interest rate hikes.

While the term "Biden malaise" effectively captures a sense of public unease and economic anxiety reminiscent of the late 1970s, a closer examination reveals that the economic realities of the two periods were not identical. The significant difference in unemployment levels, in particular, cautions against a simplistic equation of these two distinct periods. While parallels can be drawn regarding the political impact of economic anxieties and the challenge of maintaining public confidence during difficult economic times, a nuanced understanding requires acknowledging the specific economic landscapes and policy responses that characterized each era. The enduring lesson lies in the complex interplay between objective economic indicators, public perception, and the political narratives that shape our understanding of economic challenges.

American malaise ended when people began to unite with a common purpose. This shift took root during the difficult times of economic uncertainty and social unrest. Communities came together, sharing ideas and working toward solutions that would benefit everyone. Leaders emerged, inspiring hope and encouraging participation in local projects. While challenges remained, the spirit of collaboration fostered a renewed sense of optimism. This turning point ignited a desire for change, allowing citizens to believe in a brighter future and a stronger nation.

Query: American malaise ended when people began to unite with a common purpose. This shift took root during the difficult times of economic uncertainty and social unrest. Communities came together, sharing ideas and working toward solutions that would benefit everyone. Leaders emerged, inspiring hope and encouraging participation in local projects. While challenges remained, the spirit of collaboration fostered a renewed sense of optimism. This turning point ignited a desire for change, allowing citizens to believe in a brighter future and a stronger nation.

(1) Research historical periods in American history characterized by a sense of "malaise" or widespread discontent.

(2) Identify periods of significant economic uncertainty and social unrest in American history.

(3) Investigate instances where national unity and a

sense of common purpose emerged during or after such periods.

(4) Explore the specific events, challenges, or catalysts that led to this unity.

(5) Research examples of community-led initiatives and collaborative problem-solving during these turning points.

(6) Identify key leaders who emerged during these periods and analyze their role in fostering hope and encouraging participation.

(7) Examine the factors that contributed to a renewed sense of optimism and a belief in a brighter future.

(8) Analyze the long-term impact of these periods of unity and change on American society and the nation's trajectory.

Epilogue:

After going to the market, one sees our crumbling economy everyday. The Malaise of the downwardly cascading power of the US currency has made most Americans worry about what the future holds for us as a sovereign country.

Just the sticker shock of everyday food, clothing and especially property rentals in most metropolitan areas of the US have dramatically risen. After one fumbled negotiation and added regulations upon businesses, the US government has made it worse for Americans to cope with everyday essentials. Even groceries have risen to unbearable prices. In the Sixties $20.00 bought your family almost a week's worth of food to cook. Didn't America have more farmland than any other country? Where has all the overflowing bounty of food gone? Supply and demand for products have risen so aggressively both parents in a home have to work, just to make it through the year.

It feels as though we have no other opportunities. We live in a world with deep-seated angst. Families have to deal with fears in both our personal and professional survival. An all-consuming disillusionment such as this can make or break newly formed families or even one's ready for an empty nest. Your synergy will be determined by your passivity or readiness. We have seen decades of cyclic disillusionment in America. Your job will be how you govern it to make you better or let it manipulate you to fear its fallout.

Here are some ideas for you to keep in mind:
You are not the only one dealing with these occurrences. Entire nations have similar circumstances forced upon them as well. We can not control what happens in the world yet we can be ready. Even if the worst doesn't materialize you will be ready when it does. It is better to know what you do have control over and have that as a converse opportunity. Who knows being ahead of the downward curve will help your family more than just dealing with it equitably.

What do we do for the betterment of the family, neighbor-hood and society? You need to be fervent in your good ideas, exercising your inner realist that helps you become the exceptional person you need to be.

Know when you need help. Then ask the "right" people in your life to help. You will both be stronger afterward if you work together to get this job done. A great thing about being married to someone you trust and that you can lean upon regularly is that you are that team already. You have to talk about who's role will lead and the other will support. Any effort as a team will be better for your family. Separate the tasks that need to be solved and agree on what methods you both will use. This is another hurdle you have instantly overcome.

Back away for a few minutes, or a day. Consider your op-tions and what they will initially be and how they will affect your partner and family members. Think on your feet but don't dawdle. Those that let this destroy a previous great family unit will mostly likely drop into the disillusionment depression. If history doesn't show you these things work out sooner or later, then you haven't read this book too well. Be a leader, don't let circumstances pilot your endeavors.

This all seems to be a withdrawal from the Covid years. Your family is counting on you, just as your grandfather ushered his family out of the depression, and your father had to deal with the gas stranglehold on the US that almost destroyed America. Your conviction in yourself and that you will come out of this better and stronger that will make you a family chieftain.

Bibliography

- Allison Schwartz | Ben Noon (July 18, 2022) An Operation Paperclip for Taiwan. By RealClearPolicy
- Bernard Carpenter, Biden has driven America over a cliff.
- George Bush White House, the archives. (2008)
- Haidong, Li (Dec 02, 2021) When US youth is disillusioned in American democracy, how can it rekindle global passion?
- History channel Online,
- "How Washington's farewell address inspired future Presidents".
- "Losing the island of Taiwan to mainland China would represent more than the tragic death of Taiwanese democracy and a military disaster for the United States".
- "Monopoly Power Is Crushing the Soul of America" (October 27, 2023)
- "Office of the Historian" website.
- "Pew Research center" (2019)
- Vengapally, Meeta How To Overcome Disillusionment—and Succeed—in Today's America
- Multiple Internet queries on multiple information venues.
- Using today's technology (ai) led to finding information not commonly documented.

Uncommon terms requiring further clarification:

Anomie:

- is a sociological concept that refers to a condition in which society provides little moral guidance to individuals. It often arises during periods of significant social or economic upheaval, where norms break down or become unclear.

Baby Boomers:

- Grew up during a time of economic prosperity and social change. Witnessed major events like the civil rights movement, Vietnam War, moon landing, and the rise of television.
  Often portrayed as valuing hard work, individualism, and loyalty to employers. Many are now retiring or approaching retirement, which has significant economic and social implications.

Bureaucratic:

- Bureaucracy refers to a system of administration characterized by strict policies, rules, and procedures. It is often associated with government organizations but can be found in private corporations as well. Bureaucracies have a defined structure with a clear chain of command. They operate under a set of established rules and guidelines that dictate operations.

Cultural influences:

- shape individual and collective actions in profound ways, highlighting the importance of understanding cultural contexts in various fields, including education, healthcare, and social policy.

Civil Rights:

- progress for African Americans has been marked by periods of hope and regression. From the amendments during the Reconstruction era to the landmark legislation of the Civil Rights Movement, progress has been notable but remains continuously challenged. The ongoing advocacy for comprehensive social justice and equality highlights the persistent struggle that shapes the narrative of civil rights in America.

Counterculture:
- serve as crucial indicators of societal tensions and aspirations, reflecting a broader quest for authenticity, individualism, and equality in the face of established traditions and values

Disillusionment:
- Emotional Reaction: It often comes with feelings of betrayal, confusion, or even grief.
  Triggered By: Realizing a person or institution isn't what you thought (e.g., a political leader, religion, workplace). Experiencing a gap between expectations and reality (e.g., adulthood vs. childhood dreams).Seeing contradictions or hypocrisy in deeply held beliefs.

The Great Depression:
- was a transformative period that reshaped economies, societies, and political landscapes around the globe. Its legacy continues to impact economic thought and policy to this day as societies strive to prevent the recurrence of such devastating economic downturns.

Malaise:
- A general feeling of discomfort, unease, or illness, often with no identifiable cause.

Me Generation:
- s a historically and culturally specific term—primarily referring to the Baby Boomer generation (born approx-

imately 1946–1964), especially as characterized in the 1970s and 1980s, when it was perceived as self-centered, individualistic, and consumer-driven.

<u>the New Deal:</u>
- is viewed as a pivotal moment in American history, reflecting the government's commitment to addressing social issues and economic crisis through comprehensive policy responses. Its influence can still be observed in contemporary social welfare programs and the government's role in economic regulation.

Neo-liberalism:
- is a complex and influential ideology that has substantially impacted global economic practices and policies, with ongoing discussions regarding its efficacy and ethical implications.

<u>the Reconstruction Acts:</u>
- represented a landmark moment in the United States, as they outlined the conditions under which Southern states could rejoin the Union following the Civil War. By enforcing military governance and guaranteeing civil rights, these acts sought to rebuild a nation fractured by conflict. Although the efforts ultimately met with resistance and resulted in a prolonged struggle for civil rights, the Reconstruction Acts set precedents for future civil rights legislation and the ongoing pursuit of equality in America.

<u>Tet Offensive:</u>
....was a strategic failure for North Vietnam in military terms, but it was a major political and psychological victory, reshaping U.S. involvement in the Vietnam War and contributing to growing anti-war sentiment in the U.S.

Index:

249

www.ingramcontent.com/pod-product-compliance
Lightning Source LLC
Chambersburg PA
CBHW070813270326
41927CB00010B/2401